making
COUNTRY FURNITURE

making
COUNTRY FURNITURE

George Buchanan

15
STEP-BY-STEP
PROJECTS

The Taunton Press

Dedication
To ELW

ACKNOWLEDGMENTS
I would like to thank everyone who has helped me with this book,
and in particular Abigail Glover and Emma Clegg, my editors at Batsford,
Jennie Brech, Jennie Hymas and Theophilus Gimbel for letting me use their homes
for the photographs, and Elizabeth for her support, her ideas and her criticism.

Text, illustrations and designs © George Buchanan 1997
The moral right of the author has been asserted.
Photographs © B T Batsford Ltd 1997

First published in the USA in 1998 by

The Taunton Press Inc.
63 South Main Street
PO Box 5506
Newtown, CT 06470-5506
e-mail: tp@taunton.com

A catalogue record for this book is available from the British Library.

ISBN 1-56158-262-X

Library of Congress Cataloging–in–Publication Data

Buchanan, George, 1948-
    Making country furniture / George Buchanan.
        p.   cm.
    Includes index.
    ISBN 1-56158-262-X
    1. Furniture making–United States–Amateurs' manuals. 2. Country
furniture–United States–Amateurs' manuals.   I. Title.
TT195.B78 1998   97-34430
684.1'04–dc21   CIP

Printed in Singapore

Photography by Tony Boase (pages 25, 33,
73, 93, 129, 137, 148-9, 157 and 165),
Jennie Brech (pages 1, 52-3, 104-5 and 113)
and George Buchanan (pages 9, 12-13, 16, 41, 61 and 85)
Line illustrations by George Buchanan
Designed by DWN Ltd, London

CONTENTS

INTRODUCTION

The term 'country style' embraces a wide range of designs, from the clean minimal lines of a Shaker cupboard to the rustic charm of a trestle table. The beauty of country furniture lies in its timeless simplicity, its solid, homely feel. A piece of country furniture can be just as well suited to a room in the most chic and stylish town house as to the warm, mellow surroundings of a converted barn. A simple comfortable chair or useful trinket box can become a treasured possession, something to be handed down from generation to generation, valued not so much for its elegant craftsmanship but because it allows the beauty of the wood to make its own statement. Such pieces should both complement and be complemented by their surroundings. They should look as if they belong.

Country-style furniture does not have to be perfect, but it should say something about the maker and it must look accessible. These pieces were made to be used, not just looked at. The projects in this book follow and indeed celebrate the centuries-old tradition of the country woodworker who used readily available local woods to produce furniture that was more about function than fashion, that was plainer than the elegant or ornately decorated and upholstered designs popular in the towns. Country furniture produced in eighteenth- and nineteenth-century Europe and colonial America grew to have a certain style and charm of its own and is today highly sought after by antique collectors. Its enduring popularity and appeal suggests that for many it conjures up a rich heritage of tradition and creativity – to own something made years, perhaps even centuries, ago and cherished ever since is a way of owning a small piece of the past. Yet with some basic information and some helpful pointers the inspiration and skills of the past can be made to flourish well into the future.

This is intended to be a no-nonsense instruction book with projects that are easy to make and that will look good when they are finished. Although you cannot always see from the photographs, much of the furniture is nailed or screwed together. This is because I have chosen quick methods of getting results – short cuts that I know country craftsmen have taken in the past. Such methods as these are not necessarily the fine furniture maker's way, but they do work well on a practical level.

You should be able to make these pieces without having to spend a lot on tools and materials. I have assumed that you will have access to a basic workshop with a few planes, some saws, clamps, chisels and a gouge or two. Although the ladder-back chairs illustrated on page 93 look turned, they are actually fashioned with a knife and plane, so a lathe is not required. An electric circular saw and a jigsaw would be useful, but they are not essential for any of these projects.

Included in the text are hints to assist beginners; there are sections covering sharpening, sawing, planing and cutting joints. There are also some useful guidelines for finishing, which are shown at the end of each project to demonstrate that an

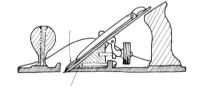

imaginative and bold finish can greatly enhance a simple piece. This is because furniture has an aesthetic function as well as a day-to-day use and by choosing the right finish it is possible to bring out the qualities of, say, ancient oak or bright cherry.

Above all, I hope that people who come to this book without any experience of woodwork will feel inspired and encouraged by the simplicity and clarity of the making processes. These days few people require a knowledge of woodwork, but I hope that those who take it up as a pastime will be richly rewarded by the sheer pleasure of making things with wood.

George Buchanan.

TOOLS AND TECHNIQUES

In the introduction I mentioned that you do not need many special tools to make the projects in this book. It is, however, important that you use good quality tools, and it is always a waste of money to buy cheap copies of good makes. Some of my hand tools are quite old, but tools of this type and quality are still readily available. My electric tools are in the Bosch DIY range. They are cheaper than the professional equivalents and, although they have a few drawbacks, they are ideal for the amateur craftsman.

SAWS

My portable circular saw and small jigsaw are part of the Bosch DIY range. I have another jigsaw that is a professional tool. I have had it for about twenty years, and it is a solid, accurate and powerful tool. When I was making the projects in this book, I used my saw table a great deal. This is another Bosch DIY tool, and I arranged an extension to the parallel fence, which allows it to be clamped at both ends, making it more rigid and improving its accuracy.

My handsaws are made by Sandvik. They are beautifully balanced tools, with taper-ground blades, which are ideal for carpentry and cabinet work. My dovetail saw is made by Tyzak, and my coping saw is by Eclipse. My fretsaw is an old one I rescued from our local scrapyard.

Circular Saw

Always wear ear defenders and proper protective spectacles when you use a circular saw.

The height of the saw blade can be adjusted by the screw under the table, and the blade can be swung to cut at angles up to 45 degrees. The parallel fence has a scope of about 6in (150mm), and the angle fence slightly less, depending on how much blade is left showing (Fig. 1). The saw comes with a coarse cut ripping blade, but for most work a stiffer, combination or general-purpose blade will be more use.

When you use the saw, have handy a couple of knotched wooden pushing sticks to hold and guide the work. These sticks will importantly keep your hands away from the blade, but they also slow down all your actions, which is a safeguard against accidents. Most accidents that occur with circular

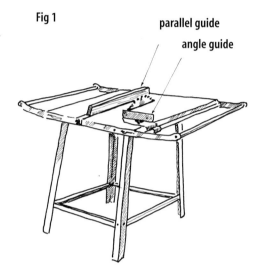

Fig 1

parallel guide

angle guide

saws seem to happen when the operator is in too much of a hurry.

A hose connected to a vacuum cleaner will extract dust – do this for any but the briefest of saw cuts.

Parallel Cuts

Adjust the fence, and clamp it tight. If you are cutting long battens, make sure that there is adequate support on the exit side, at the same level as, or slightly below, the level of the saw table. Control the piece that you are sawing with both hands, but when your hands reach the saw table, pick up your pushing sticks and finish the cut using the sticks to control the workpiece. Remember never to

Making a parallel saw cut, using pushing sticks.

allow your hands onto the saw table when the saw is running.

Angle Cuts

Swing the angle guide into position. In most DIY saws there is some play in this fence, and you should practise a way of holding and guiding the work to give the best results. Pushing one-handed, from the centre of the guide, seems to work best.

When you need to make an accurate start to the cut, mark the line of the saw on the table. You can scribe the line with a straightedge or put a piece of masking tape on the table and mark it with a ball-point pen.

Repetitive Cuts

To cut several short lengths, clamp a block to the table or parallel guide to give an accurate endstop and feed the wood against the stop, before pushing the wood, supported by the guide, across the blade (Fig. 2). For longer work, arrange an extension on the angled guide and clamp a stop to it (see page 140, where this is described in greater detail for the Twelve-drawer Chest).

Fig 2

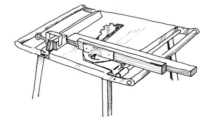

Rebates

Set the height of the blade and the parallel fence. Feed the work over the blade, pressing down hard and keeping the work against the fence. For large rebates you will need to reset the saw and fence and make the second releasing cut (see page 69, where this is described in the making of the Kneehole Desk).

Grooves

Mark the groove on a test piece. Set the fence and the height of the saw, and then run the workpiece over the blade. To increase the width of the groove, move the parallel guide and make another pass.

Portable Circular Saws

One of my two portable saws (Fig. 3) is permanently mounted beneath the saw table, where it is in regular use. I use the other outside the workshop for cutting large, rough-sawn boards to size. This type of saw is held with two hands, and for most rough converting work you can sight the line you are cutting through a slot in the saw table.

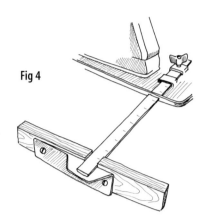

Fig 4

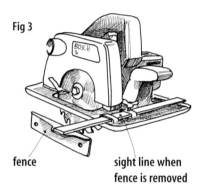

Fig 3

fence

sight line when
fence is removed

These hand-held saws are powerful and cut quickly through heavy timber, and if you are not used to using them, their energy can be a little alarming. They are a great asset when you need to convert large or unevenly edged boards because you can reduce the wood to manageable sizes without having to lift them across the saw table.

If you have a machined straightedge to work from, you can use the adjustable parallel guide, but if you are sawing thin board, it is advisable to adapt the fence slightly by screwing a wooden strip to the fence (Fig. 4). This gives a longer bearing face and prevents the board from riding up over the edge of the fence.

Use the saw with the blade set to minimum depth. It is easier to control and you are less likely to saw the trestles in half. Most good portable electric saws are fitted with a safety fence that retracts automatically when the saw is slid onto the workpiece. Once you start the saw, hold it tightly with both hands.

Steering the saw along a pencil line is not a particularly accurate way of sawing. If there is no straightedge to use with the parallel guide, find a straight batten and tack it to the workpiece and use that to guide the saw.

Jigsaws

The jigsaw (Fig. 5) does everything and more that a bow saw, a coping saw and pad saw can do, and it works faster.

The jigsaws illustrated in Fig. 5 have a variable speed control and an arrangement that allows you to vary the orbital action of the blade. The orbital action has the effect of pulling the saw along the board. This reduces both the amount of feed pressure required and the tendency of the blade to wander off the vertical.

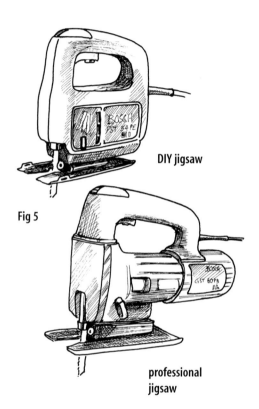

DIY jigsaw

Fig 5

professional
jigsaw

Set the orbital action to zero as you meet another cut, otherwise the forward-moving blade will score the wood you are approaching.

A variety of blades is available to suit most purposes. For these projects, I used the following:
• for straight cuts: T 101D
• for straight clean cuts: T 101BR
• for curves: T 244D
• for tight corners: T 119BO

Handsaws

I use two handsaws – a rip saw, with large (5ppi), square-cut teeth, and a cross-cut saw, with much smaller, knifelike teeth. The rip saw is used for cuts along the grain, and the cross-cut saw for cuts in other directions and fine work.

Generally, these saws are held with one hand, with the index finger pointing down the blade. It is tempting to use both hands to apply more force and downward pressure, but this makes the saw less accurate. Most cuts are made with the saw held at 45 degrees to the surface being sawn. Because the blade is flexible, the points of the teeth can be positioned exactly where you want them. Small adjustments to the line of cut are easy to make, and with practice you will soon be able to cut down a line accurately.

Keeping the blade vertical is a different matter. Starting at a corner of the board, you will have two marks to work from. From then on, you cannot rely on the blade to keep the cut square, and you need to check the blade regularly with a set square.

The blade will sometimes obscure your view of the marks – especially when you are sawing tenons – and you will have to peer over the blade to see what is happening. Figs. 6 and 7 show the different viewpoints you might need when you are sawing tenons.

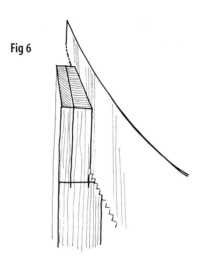

Fig 6

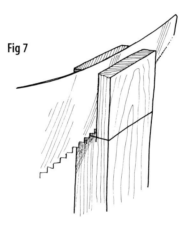

Fig 7

Tenon Saws and Dovetail Saws

The fine-toothed blades of these small saws are backed by mild steel or brass strips to keep them rigid. They are used for cutting the shoulders of tenons, for dovetails and for other small, accurate work. They are held with one hand, while the other usually props the work against the bench hook.

To make an accurate cut across the grain, mark the line with a knife, use the edge of a sharp chisel to pare away a shaving on the waste side of the line and then lodge the saw in the shallow groove and saw downwards from there (Figs. 8 and 9).

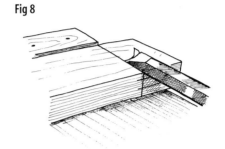

Fig 8

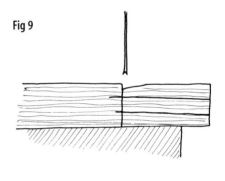

Fig 9

Coping Saws and Bow Saws

Both these saws, which are held with both hands, have narrow blades that are tensioned by the frame of the saw. The blades can be swivelled to execute complex cuts up to about 5in (125mm) from the edge of the plank.

I usually prefer to arrange the blades so that they cut on the push stroke. When you adjust the angle of the blade, make sure that the blade is not twisted when you begin sawing.

Variable speed jigsaw.

Sawing down a tenon.

Removing the waste.

ROUTER

You do not need a router in your workshop, but once you have one you will wonder how you managed without. Mine is illustrated in Fig. 10, and I use it for mortising and for running mouldings.

Wear safety spectacles and ear defenders, and clean the floor and bench between operations. Keep your cutters sharp. TC and HSS cutters can be honed on the inside edge with a fine oil stone.

CHISELS

You should have at least five chisels in your workshop. The ones that I find the most useful are three bevel-edge chisels, ⅝in (16mm), ⅜in (10mm) and ¼in (6mm), and two mortise chisels, ¼in (6mm) and 3/8in (10mm) (Fig. 11).

Fig 10

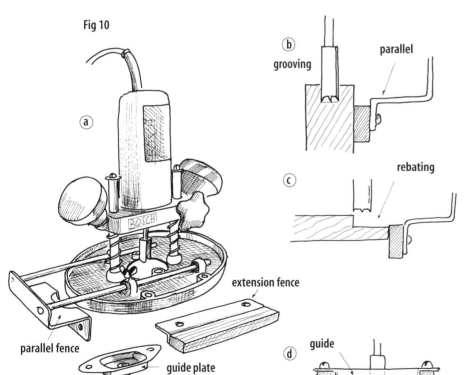

parallel fence
guide plate
extension fence
template
guide
workpiece

(a)
(b) grooving — parallel
(c) rebating
(d)

Fig 11

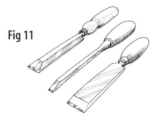

Bevel-edge chisels are delicate tools, used for paring and trimming. They should be as sharp as you can manage to get them because the sharper they are, the easier and, therefore, safer they are to use.

Mortise chisels are designed to withstand the levering and malletting required to work mortises deep into hardwood. These, too, need to be very sharp (see page 13).

Firmer chisels are square-sectioned, strong tools. The 1½in (38mm) chisel shown opposite is the only one I use frequently.

A carefully controlled slice.

Chisels are always useful, and you may occasionally come across them in junk shops. Provided the blades are not pitted, they should be serviceable. If you collect more than one bevel-edge or firmer chisel, ½ in (12mm) wide, grind the end of one to about 60 degrees, and grind the sharpening bevel to make a matching pair. Use for carving or for cutting lapped dovetails.

Hold as in the photograph below. The fingers of the left hand guide restrain the blade, while the right hand grips the handle and presses forwards. When you are mortising, the left hand holds the chisel, and the right the mallet. This allows you to check that the chisel is perpendicular.

A firmer chisel.

Sharpening

Although I have a grindstone in my workshop, I have found that a faceplate, covered with 100 grit abrasive paper and mounted in the lathe is faster and gives an equally good edge.

If you use a grindstone, the tool is normally fed against the direction of rotation, but when you use a faceplate, the edge is dragged against the revolving disc (Fig. 12). Grind the edge to the angle, taking care not to overheat the blade. When you use a high-speed grindstone it is useful to have a small tub of water handy in which you can rest your tools to allow them to cool.

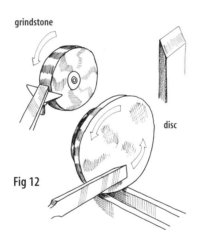

grindstone

disc

Fig 12

The next stage is to use a coarse sharpening stone. Lubricate it with light oil, and, holding the blade at the angle shown, slide it back and forth over the stone, counting slowly to five (Fig. 13). If you run your finger lightly up the back of the blade, you will feel a slight ragged burr. Turn the tool over and flat it

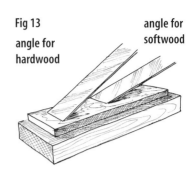

Fig 13
angle for
hardwood

angle for
softwood

against the stone to remove the burr, counting one. Repeat this a couple of times, applying diminishing pressure.

Lubricate a fine stone and repeat, each time raising a burr and slicing it off with the back of the blade flat against the stone. Finish on a stropping board, stroking the blade in the same proportions of 5:1.

For sharpening plane blades you will need a curved slipstone to remove the inside burr (Fig. 14).

The sharpening bevel is ground with a rocking action, which wears a groove in the sharpening stone. The groove makes it difficult to use

Fig 14

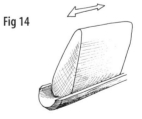

the stone for sharpening planes and chisels, which have almost straight cutting edges, and it is a good idea to keep a separate sharpening stone for gouges.

PLANES, SCRAPERS AND SANDPAPER

I have three planes that I use all the time. They are a 22in (560mm) jointer plane, a 9½in (240mm) smoothing plane and a 6¼in (160mm) block plane, which is excellent for delicate work and for trimming end grain. I also use a 3:1 rebate plane and an 'improved' shoulder rebate plane, which is about 8½in (216mm) long and narrower than the 3:1.

Blunt planes are punishing to use. Always keep the blades well honed, and if you find the work difficult, reduce the amount of blade that is showing and lubricate the sole with candlewax.

For rough and rapid removal of stock, open the mouth of the plane and raise the cap iron slightly (Fig. 15). For fine work, close the mouth and lower the cap iron until it is at the very edge of the plane iron.

Planes should be stored on their sides or with their soles raised to lift the blade off the shelf.

Fig 15

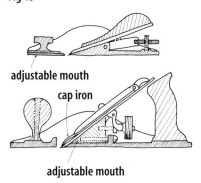

adjustable mouth
cap iron
adjustable mouth

Jointing a Surface

Fig. 16 shows the slightly curved blade, just proud of the smooth, flat bottom of the plane. Although this curve is exaggerated, a gentle curve is desirable and a great help when you are shooting joints. When the blade is set as illustrated, the shaving will be thicker at the centre of the blade than at the edges.

Fig 16

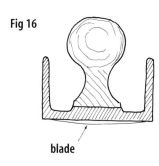

blade

After you have planed the edge of the board straight (using a jointer plane), you still have to plane it square. Check the edge and mark the high spots on the joining edge. Steer the centre of the plane blade over the high spots to render the edge level. Keep the sole flat on the edge – there is no need to tilt it – and move the plane sideways as you approach the different high spots (Fig. 17).

Fig 17

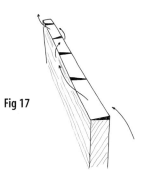

If you still cannot make a satisfactory joint, rub blackboard chalk on one edge and rub the joining edge to it. Take a block plane and ease off the chalk marks.

Levelling a Board

Sight down the board using winding sticks (Fig. 18) to help identify the high spots. Prop the board against the bench stop and, if necessary, tack some battens around it to stop it sliding about. If the board does not lie flat on the bench, wedge slivers of wood or card beneath it.

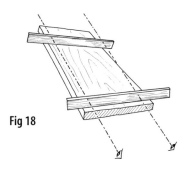

Fig 18

Use a long plane with the blade set fine to remove the high spots. Plane diagonally, altering angles regularly. As the board is levelled, draw back the blade until only the finest shavings are removed, then finish with a scraper.

Scraper

A scraper is an effective smoothing tool even when you are working with contrary and confused grain. It is less effective on softwood such as deal and spruce. The scraper is held as illustrated in Fig. 19, sprung into a slight curve by the thumbs. Altering the angle of the scraper will allow you to vary the width and the depth of the cut.

Fig 19 scraper

Sharpening

When the scraper becomes difficult to use, sharpen it. The cutting edges of a scraper (and they are sharpened on all sides) are actually small hooks. Sometimes the hooks can be restored simply by running a sharp point, such as the point of a masonry nail, along the hook to clear it. If this doesn't work you must sharpen it.

Place the scraper on its side and remove the hooks with an oilstone (Fig. 20). Place the scraper in the vice, edge upwards, and, holding a fine flat file at right angles to its sides, file the edge flat (Fig. 21). One or two passes of the file will be quite enough for this. You can tell when the scraper is ready for the next stage by feeling the corner of the edge: it should be sharp enough to rasp your skin.

Take a burnishing tool or the polished back of a gouge and make a couple of passes along the edge. Each time the angle is slightly more

Fig 20

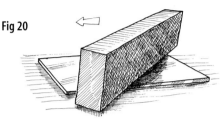

Fig 21

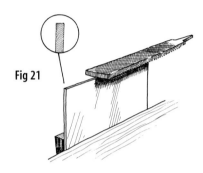

acute. Press quite hard, and move the burnishing tool downwards as well as across the edge (Fig. 22). The scraper is now ready for use.

Fig 22

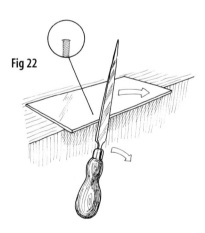

SANDERS AND SANDPAPER

Fig. 23 shows three electric sanders, all of which I find extremely useful. The belt sander is ideal for smoothing large surfaces, the orbital

Fig 23 multi-sander

belt

orbital

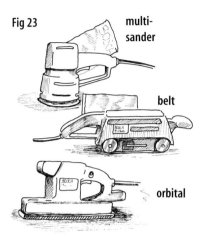

sander is an excellent, labour-saving finishing tool, and the eccentric multi-sander is useful for both rough shaping and finishing. These are easy tools to use, but you must remember to wear a dust mask when you are using them. The fine dust generated by these high-speed sanders is a health hazard.

Sandpaper comes in different grades of roughness, indicated by a number – the higher the number, the smoother the paper. The finest grade I use is about 240 grit, and 60 grit is the roughest. Intermediate grades of 180 (fine), 120 and 100 (medium fine) are the most often used, and you should keep a few sheets of 500 grit for rubbing down a French-polished finish.

Sanding by hand should be carried out at a slight angle to the grain. Start with the coarsest paper and use the sanding block at about 30 degrees to the direction of the grain. This will level the harder, darker grain without unduly scouring the softer summer growth

(Fig. 24). Reduce the angle when you change to medium grit, and remove all the marks left by the coarse grit paper. Finish using the fine papers parallel with the grain.

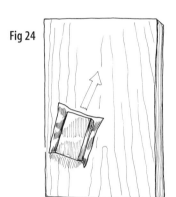

Fig 24

Using a gauge.

If you are sanding an assembled framed panel, sand the mouldings first, then the panel, then the rails (horizontals) and finally the stiles (verticals).

Setting Out and Marking Out

The tools that you will normally need comprise two set squares, one mitre bevel and an adjustable sliding bevel, several marking and cutting gauges, and a mortise gauge, two pairs of compasses, a marking knife and a tape measure. You will also need a wooden straightedge and a pointed batten to check diagonals.

When you wish to identify an adjacent squared edge and side, mark them with the symbols shown in Fig. 25. When you are scribing a shoulder line around a squared-up

Marking a shoulder with a knife.

length of wood, lodge the point of your knife in the nick left in the corner of the wood caused by the previous cut, and draw the set square up against it. This guarantees an accurate continuation of the line.

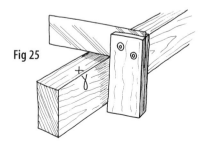

Fig 25

If you are squaring around a piece that has only one pair of adjacent faces known to be at right angles, square them using the known true faces to bear the set square against.

SLIDING BEVEL

It is sometimes handy to have more than one sliding bevel (Fig. 26). If you have only one, keep a spare block of wood on which you can record angles that you will need again. Mark them with a knife or sharp pencil.

Fig 26

GAUGES

These are used as illustrated (Fig. 27). Some pressure is needed to control these tools, and it is usually worthwhile fixing the workpiece in the vice to mark it.

Fig 27

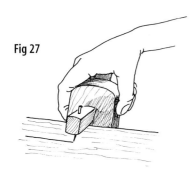

The cutting gauge is home-made, and its knife is made from a ground-down jigsaw blade. It is easy to make and well worth the trouble. Cutting gauges are particularly useful for setting out hinges and cutting veneers prior to fitting stringing or cross-banding. If you choose to make your own, cut out the fence and finish it before fitting the stock that slides through it. Fit the knife and wedges last (Fig. 28).

Fig 28

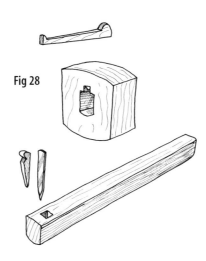

DIVIDERS AND DUMBSTICKS

When a piece of timber has to be shaped to fit against an irregular structure, the shape can be transferred with a rectangular dumbstick or a pair of dividers locked to the appropriate setting (Fig. 29). Remember that the offsets marked off must all be parallel with each other or the marking out will be inaccurate.

Fig 29

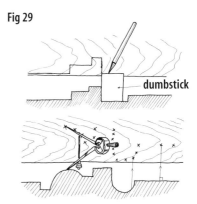

dumbstick

dividers set at maximum distance and held perpendicular

HAMMERS, NAILS, PUNCHES AND PINCERS

Apart from one or two heavy old ball-pein, metalworking hammers and my two wooden carving mallets, I have only two hammers, and they are both Warrington pattern, which has a cross-pein behind the head for starting nails. One is a pin hammer and the other a medium weight hammer. The pincers are for pulling out the bent nails.

The larger the nail, the bigger the hammer you will need. The pin hammer is used for hammering sewing pins (with their heads snipped off), panel and veneer pins. The larger hammer is used with heavier nails – wire and galvanized wire nails, lost heads and ovals. These are usually sufficiently long for the cross-pein not to be needed for starting nails off, but the cross-pein makes an excellent veneer hammer for rubbing down cross-banding (see Veneering, page 167).

Fig 30

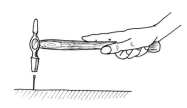

Hold the hammer as illustrated (Fig. 30), and lower the end of the handle slightly as the nail is driven home. Hammering in nails is not as easy as it looks. Do not hammer a nail flush. Although the face of the hammer is slightly domed, one day you will mishit, and the hammer will leave an indelible and most unwelcome impression in the wood. Use a punch to drive in the nail head and choose a punch of the right size – a small pin punch for pins and heavier punches for nails.

Support the piece you are hammering. Nails usually bend when there is no direct support behind them. If necessary ask a helper to hold a heavy wooden block or hammer to absorb the impact. I have several metal dollies, gleaned from all sorts of places, for this purpose.

Keep the face of the hammer clean. PVA glue is especially slippery, and if it gets onto the face of the hammer, the nail will slide and bend. Clean the face regularly by drawing the hammer across a scrap of rough sandpaper.

It is often difficult to hold short pins steady while you hit them, and they are sometimes too thin for the cross-pein to be much use. Instead, grip the pin in the jaws of some long-nosed pliers and tap the pin head.

When you need to pull out a nail, grip the shank with pincers, protecting the workpiece by laying a thin strip of wood beneath the pincer's jaws, and lever out the nail. The pincer jaws are sharp but not

Fig 31

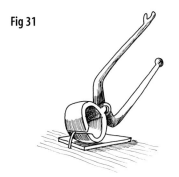

usually sharp enough to cut through the nail (Fig. 31).

Hammers are generally more useful than mallets for knocking joints apart. Before hitting the joint, protect it from damage with a straight and substantial batten.

SCREWDRIVERS AND SCREWS

You will only need two types of screws – countersunk woodscrews and twin-thread screws – for making the projects described in this book (Fig. 32).

Countersunk screws require three drilling operations before they

Fig 32

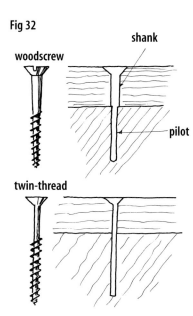

can be fitted – a narrow pilot hole, which is the full depth of the screw plus head, a wider shank hole, which is the diameter of the unthreaded part of the shank, and a conical depression, which is drilled by a special countersinking rose bit.

Twin-thread screws require one drilling operation – for the pilot hole, and in softwood, even that is not always necessary. Twin-threads can be bought with cross-heads, which are easier to drive using an electric drill, or with slots.

Both types of screw have their advantages. Twin-thread screws are quick and easy to fix and, provided the work is well clamped before screwing, pull the work up tight.

Traditional countersunk screws look better. The heads lie flush with the wood, there is little or no distortion of the grain around them, and their narrow machined slots look tidy, especially when they are lined up. In addition, these screws are better for pulling joints together, and unlike twin-thread screws, it is unnecessary to clamp them before screwing. I use countersunk woodscrews where the heads will be seen. Elsewhere I am inclined to use twin-threads.

Whatever the screw, it is important to use a suitable screwdriver. The blade of the screwdriver should fit the slot of the screw. If it is too big, it will score the surface of the wood; if it is too narrow, it will chew the slot. This is equally important with cross-heads: the screwdriver must slip neatly into the screw and withdraw easily, particularly if you are using a drill to drive the screws. If there is a tendency to bind, you will either break the tangs on the screwdriver or drive the screws in too far.

USING AN ADZE

The adze must be razor sharp if it is to be useful. Use both hands to grip the handle close to its end and allow a limited, easy swing. Hold the wood with the heels of your shoes or with a block braced against a wall. Cut across the grain or at an angle to the grain.

Start with the tip of the blade just touching the surface of the wood. Swing the head up until it is about 12in (300mm) of arc from where it will strike the wood. Allow it to swing back, adding a little

impetus with your wrists. Gradually increase the force you apply. To begin with, practise removing thin shavings, no more than 1in (25mm) wide and $\frac{1}{16}$in (1mm) thick. Once you have developed a feel for the tool you will be able to take slices almost $\frac{1}{8}$in (2mm) thick, and 3in (75mm) or more broad.

Work across the plank and then change your position further along.

FOXED PEGS

To be effective these pegs should be at least $\frac{1}{2}$in (12mm) in diameter. If you know you will need foxed pegs, be on the look out for offcuts that have a particularly straight grain. Saw the offcuts to length – 3–4in (75–100mm) – and remember where you store them.

To make a peg, take the side axe and a hammer. Hold the axe in position, resting on the offcut, and strike it with the hammer (Fig. 33).

Fig 33

Trim the pegs again with the axe – they should be slightly oversize, tapered and have angular corners.

Riving the pegs like this almost guarantees that the grain of the peg

will run true. Careful wedging will not break the peg, and it will withstand a lot of hammering.

Split the pegs to size. Whittle an abrupt point at one end of the peg and make a thin saw cut into its end, extending downwards by 1in (25mm) (Fig. 34). Split some hardwood wedges, 1in (25mm) long and no more than $\frac{3}{32}$in (1.5mm) wide at their widest. Trim them sharp and smooth with a chisel as they are pressed against the bench hook (Fig. 35).

Fig 34
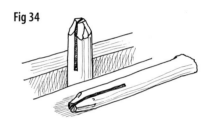

Fig 35
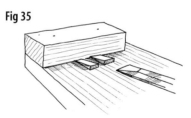

Bore the hole for the peg $\frac{1}{4}$in (6mm) shorter than the peg. Slip the wedge into the end of the peg, and poke the peg into the hole. Tap in lightly and then drive it fully home with a few hard taps (Fig. 36).

Fig 36
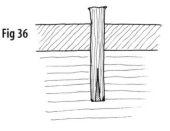

ADHESIVES

With one exception, the glue I used in all the projects described in this book is PVA adhesive. I used epoxy resin for the Sleigh Bed.

PVA Adhesive

PVA glue is a versatile water-based glue – with added water and dry colours it makes paint, unthinned it is a tough but not weatherproof adhesive.

Splashes of PVA adhesive – and other adhesives – left on the surface of the wood will resist stain, which makes finishing difficult. When you are making complex jobs it is often worthwhile staining and polishing the work before gluing. With simple projects, such as those in this book, wash off glue splashes with warm water and a stiff brush and dab the area dry.

PVA is slippery and some butt joints are difficult to clamp without the pieces sliding out of position. It is easy to overcome the problem by driving a few nails into one jointing face, and snipping off their heads close to the surface. The small pointed ends poking above the glue help locate the joining piece and stop it sliding as clamps are wound tight.

PVA contains a large percentage of water, which causes the wood to swell. The trapped water makes it difficult to clamp wide boards face to face, and the joint will take a long time to go off and the resulting join

will be patchy. In these circumstances – the Sleigh Bed is an example – I prefer to use epoxy resin, which contains no water and does not depend on evaporation to cure.

The water present in the glue can make tight-fitting joints rather difficult to press together and, once together, difficult to separate. The moisture swells the wood fibres, causing the joint to close up, and unless assembly is quick, there can be difficulties. It is a good idea to plan the gluing procedures carefully, making sure that all the necessary clamps and pads are close to hand before you start.

Using PVA Adhesive to Make Paint

I have a range of powdered earth colours and water-soluble paste colours, which are invaluable for making paints and stains. Mix the pigments before adding the glue because the white of the PVA alters the tone of the colour, which will dry darker. PVA adhesive is almost transparent when it is dry. Thin with water as necessary.

Epoxy Resin Glue

This is a two-part product, which, when mixed in the correct ratio, forms a brittle, strong and weatherproof bond. Add fine sanding dust to the mixed-up resin to fill gaps up to ¼in (6mm) without loss of strength. Epoxy resin has the advantage over PVA glue of not

shrinking as it dries. Before you use the glue apply barrier cream to your hands or wear protective gloves. Flexible plastic mixing tubs can be re-used after the glue has set.

The adhesive is composed of a resin and a separate hardener, which must be mixed in the correct ratio. Once mixed, the adhesive has to be used in a specified time. As the resin cures, it heats up slightly, gels and hardens rapidly, achieving full strength after two or three days, depending on temperature. The warming up of the resin as the two parts react together further accelerates the reaction. This exothermic effect can be minimized by working in a cold workshop, by placing the tub of mixed resin in a dish of cold water or by pouring the mixed resin into a paint tray, which dissipates the heat.

Prepare the surfaces for epoxy resin in the same way as for PVA glue. The wood must be well seasoned; the resin works best when wood has a moisture content of 18 per cent or less; and the work must be dry and grease free. Curing times vary with temperature, and the type of hardener. Using a medium or slow hardener at normal room temperature, the mixed resin has a pot life of about 30 minutes before it begins to gel, and because its pot life is so limited, I mix small quantities at a time.

Unlike PVA glue, which performs best when there is no

perceptible gap in the glue join (so clamping pressure is an advantage), epoxy relies on a film of glue between the joining pieces for its strength. Additives such as colloidal silica and cotton fibres can be mixed into the resin both to bulk out the quantity with no loss of glued strength and to prevent the resin migrating into the timber, leaving a glue-starved joint. If you are buying resin from one of the suppliers listed at the back of the book, buy some of these fillers as well, and keep them in an airtight container – they will almost double your quantity of usable resin.

WOODS

Most of the pieces of furniture illustrated in this book were made from deal, a low-grade timber, planed on all sides. I bought it from a local builders' merchant, which stores wood under cover out of doors. I use the wood direct from the yard and expect some shrinkage once the piece is brought into the house from the workshop. If you want to reduce the amount of shrinkage to the minimum, bring the wood indoors for a week or two, and stack it horizontally, with sticks between the layers of planks. After this secondary conditioning there should be little subsequent movement.

I also used cherry, ash, yew wood, oak and parana pine. Of these, the ash and the oak were only partially seasoned, and some movement and uneven shrinkage was the result. These hardwoods were bought from a local wood yard, where I purchased the planks as waney edged boards. When you buy wood in this form, you must understand that not all the wood will be useful. The sapwood and bark at the edges is of little use, and often the heartwood will be split or badly cupped. You will need to carry away from the yard considerably more wood than you expect to use, but it will probably cost you less than you thought, particularly if you negotiate the price down for flaws in the timber, wastage and so forth.

Trees are normally cut through and through, and stacked as sawn. Fig. 37 shows the types of planks you can expect to obtain from such a tree and indicates the way they will shrink. In effect, planks will shrink in the direction of the annual rings, as exposed at the end of the

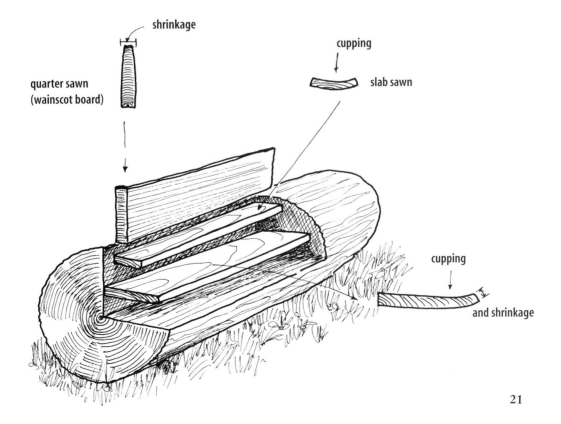

quarter sawn
(wainscot board)

shrinkage

cupping

slab sawn

cupping

and shrinkage

plank. Those rings closest to the outside of the trunk will shrink more than those at the centre, so differential shrinkage in all but the wainscot boards (cut on the quarter in the centre of the log) means that some cupping is the inevitable consequence of drying out. Longitudinal shrinkage in sound wood is negligible and can be safely ignored.

Freshly sawn hardwood planks stored outside under cover need approximately one year per inch of thickness to dry out. Immediately before use, they should be stored in a warm room for a week or two to stabilize. I enjoy using partially seasoned wood because it is easy to work and I like the surface effects produced by a limited amount of shrinkage. For example, a knotty surface planed perfectly smooth, will present a slightly knobbly appearance when it is dry.

If you know how wood will shrink, it is possible to plan which way up to position the boards you are going to use. Narrow planks will not cup much and, if they do, cupping may not be noticeable, but broader planks will cup and they are often impossible to hold flat.

Faults

Part of the interest in woodworking is coping with the faults in the wood, and if you enjoy using the interesting, knotty scraps of wood with swirling grain for highly visible

parts of the furniture, you will need to know what to look out for and how to cope with the problems.

Large knots are both unsightly and troublesome. They are the focus of adjacent confused and dense grain, and they often represent a considerable weakening of the plank. If the knot is large and going to be in a prominent place, I usually knock it out, remove the old black bark lining the hole, and fill the space by hammering in small, tapered wooden pegs of the same timber. If you force in enough pegs and wait for the glue to dry, the resulting mosaic of end-grain hexagons makes a more agreeable substitute. Alternatively, for regularly shaped knots it is easy to insert a

patch (see Graving or Patching a Plank, pages 119-120).

I leave small knots, although loose ones should be glued in place early, at the marking out stage of the construction. Try to avoid knots in areas where you will be carving a moulding or cutting a joint.

Cut off the split ends of a plank before the plank is used. If you notice traces of splitting further up the plank, which might open when the furniture is moved into a warm, dry atmosphere, make a dovetail key (Fig. 38). The key, which is made from a piece of straight-grained, well-seasoned hardwood, is laid across the split, marked around with a knife and the recess is excavated with a router or chisel.

Fig 38

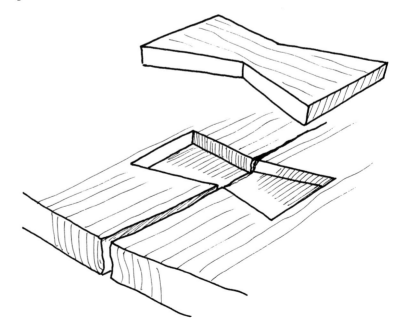

The final cuts are made with a bevel-edge chisel, held vertically, and cutting right down the incision line. This is easy once you get the hang of lodging the blade in the incision and rocking one edge down. Once the cut is started, subsequent cuts can be braced against the fresh straightedge, with only about ¼in (6mm) of the chisel lodged in the line.

Reaction wood is caused in a number of ways, but it is due to the reaction of a living tree to difficult or harsh growing conditions. Trees growing on a steep slope often have reaction wood in the lower sections of the trunk. On the uphill side, tension wood resists the inclination of the tree to lean down the slope, and it is often revealed by serious splitting at the end of the plank. When it is sawn, the waste will snake away from the blade, and the remaining plank will adopt the opposite curve. Compression timber is formed in some species of trees on the downhill side of the trunk. This wood is dense, but weak. Identifying reaction wood is not always easy. A fluffy surface after machining is one sign, and so, in a waney edged board, is an off-centre heart.

You will soon spot a piece of reaction wood when you start to work it. As you saw, it will clamp up on the saw blade and stall the saw, or spring apart once a saw cut is started, and it will be almost impossible to machine smooth. Such wood should be used for bottom boards or back planking, but not for framing and never for doors.

Wood that is bought ready planed will reveal all its faults at first glance. Reject planks that are twisted, curved or have a rough and furry edge, and also those with large knots. If you can, ask the retailer to unwrap shrink-wrapped boards before you buy. Most are likely to be usable, but you might be able to eliminate rogue planks before you pay for them.

Storing Wood

Freshly cut wood should be stacked out of doors, in the shade. Planks should be raised off the ground and supported on blocks, with battens between. Stack the planks, on top of each other, interposing thin battens between each, at intervals of about 2 feet (600mm).

Line the battens up vertically so that the loads are distributed downwards onto the concrete blocks. Cover the top with some old boards, corrugated iron, or plastic sheet, ensuring as you do that air can circulate and rainwater can drain from the stack. Paint the ends of the planks with a thick oil-based paint to inhibit drying and to prevent splits at the ends of the planks. It is important that air should circulate freely through the stack, so cut down weeds and undergrowth regularly.

Conditioning Wood

Wood that is stored and seasoned out of doors will need further drying before it is converted into furniture. There are several ways of doing this, but the way I prefer is to cut and smooth all the timber that will be used for a new project, and store the planks in the house, somewhere out of the way. Planks should be left for a couple of weeks to dry. Planks more than 1 in (25mm) thick will need longer.

After this secondary conditioning, the wood should have stabilized, and truing up and thicknessing can be carried out without any great danger of serious movement.

Woodworm

Wood should not be left stacked out of doors indefinitely. After a few years, worm will attack the sapwood, and the heartwood will be vulnerable. Make an effort not to accumulate wood that you will not use. I find it is a useful – although perhaps expensive – rule that if you do not know what you have in your wood store, you might as well throw it out.

HANGING RACK

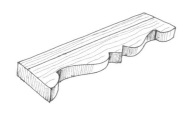

Within 'country furniture' there are quite a few different varieties of hanging rack. Fine racks for displaying crockery, often with elegant cornices, were built in Britain and America in the late eighteenth century. You will find many today in antique shops made from thin planks, often little more than ¼in (6mm) thick, and some with doors on the bottom shelf dating from the early twentieth century.

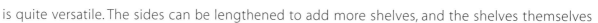

This useful yew rack is not only simple to make, but its design is quite versatile. The sides can be lengthened to add more shelves, and the shelves themselves

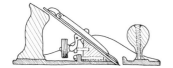

can be extended so that it can carry more books. Its simple construction and minimal decoration achieve a surprisingly graceful appearance despite its thick and heavy materials.

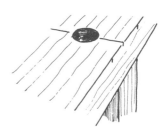

METHOD

1   Make a template of one side of the rack, using the plan drawing shown on page 31. Scale up your cardboard template to full size by transferring it to a grid where each square is 1in sq (2.5cm sq) (see Special Skills).

Use the template to mark out the two sides. With a little juggling you will find they fit quite economically onto a single plank (Fig. 1). Cut out the sides with a jigsaw and smooth the saw cuts with a half-round file or with 100 grit sandpaper wrapped around a curved block.

Fig 1

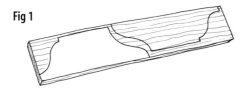

2   Mark out and cut the shelves and the frieze plank to length. They must be sawn accurately at right angles in all planes because the butt joints will be visible. A circular saw is best for this purpose (see Saws, page 8). The three shelves must be exactly the same length. Use the angle fence to trim one end of each shelf. If you have difficulty using your circular saw to cut accurate right angles, see page 11 for hints on sawing accurately by hand.

Having cut one end of each shelf, fix an endstop on your guide and, with the freshly sawn ends against the stop, saw the opposite ends (Fig. 2). This should guarantee that all four pieces are the same length.

Fig 2

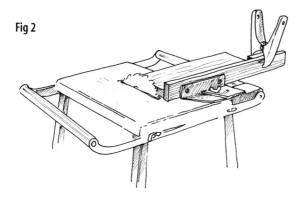

3   Make a template for the frieze and cut it out (Fig. 3). Sand the sawn edges smooth and remove any sharp corners. If the frieze board is wider than necessary, cut it to the correct width and plane its top edge smooth (see Tip, page 28).

Fig 3

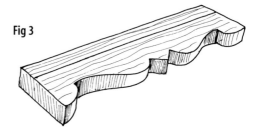

4   Place the two sides together (Fig. 4) and pencil in the position of each shelf. Square across the planks. Mark the centre line of each shelf on the outward face of both side pieces lightly in pencil (Fig. 5).

Fig 4

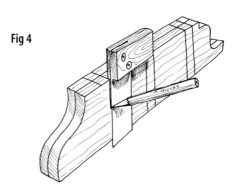

Fig 5

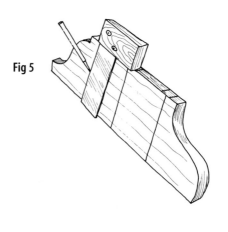

5 To secure the shelves to the sides it is best to use twin-thread screws with a parallel shank and a smaller head for their length than the traditional screw. Choose 2½in (65mm) countersunk screws with slotted heads. Each screw requires two holes – one to sink the head and a thin pilot hole to lead it into the shelf (see Special Skills). The frieze is held in the same way (though with 2in (50mm) screws) and this can be prepared at the same time. Once the components are screwed together, pegs can be used to conceal the screw heads (Fig. 6).

Fig 6

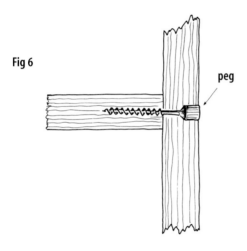

peg

6 When the sides are counterbored and ready, you can assemble the rack. Fix the top shelf first. Place it in the vice and apply a little glue to the end grain. Place the side plank across it and align it carefully. Hold it in position by tapping a thin nail through one hole while you screw the other (Fig. 7). Remove the nail and screw the second hole. Repeat for the bottom shelf. Turn over the rack, place the opposite side in position on the ends of the shelves and secure it in the same way as the first but do not pull it up quite tight. Check that it is square and correct if necessary. You may wish to tack a diagonal batten across the back to hold it square while the centre shelf is installed.

Fig 7

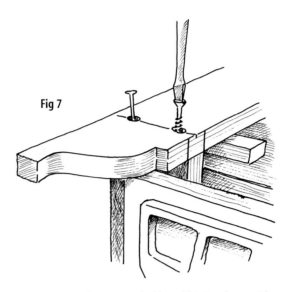

7 Position the centre shelf. Hold it in place with two nails in one end and a third nail at the other, and screw the fourth hole. Replace nails with screws and tighten all the screws. Glue and screw the frieze in place and leave to dry. Finally, cut a number of wooden pegs/plugs (see Special Skill) and insert them to conceal the screws.

FINISHING

The rack shown was finished in the same way as the candle box (see page 36) but stained with a mixture of English light oak, Canadian cedar and a small quantity of American walnut. When this was dry, I applied two coats of shellac button polish and, again, when it was dry, rubbed down the surface with 240 glasspaper dipped in linseed oil. The linseed oil was wiped off carefully with a clean cloth and three or four rubbers of shellac were applied, first in a circular motion, changing to long ovals and then to straight strokes on the last application, to smooth and fill the surface (see page 170). Several days later, when the polish had fully hardened, I rubbed it down with 0000 grade wire wool and applied a coat of brown wax.

TIP

DIY circular saws are often supplied with thin, rip sawing teeth designed to make a rough quick cut along the grain. They are useful, but better still is a general-purpose or combination blade, which can make clean cuts across the grain as well as ripping down it.

Take care when you are using the parallel fence that it is set correctly. If the fence is on the waste side of the blade, the setting of the fence should include the full width of the saw cut (Fig. 8).

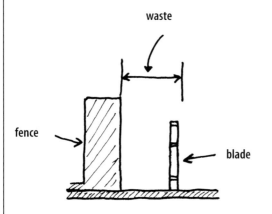

Fig 8

SPECIAL SKILLS

TRANSFERRING CURVES

Fig. 9 shows how to transfer the curved side of the rack onto a grid drawn to scale on a piece of card to provide a useful template.

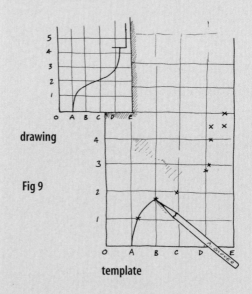

drawing

Fig 9

template

It might help to number the lines on one axis and letter the lines on the other. Then simply plot a number of points on the full-size grid which correspond to intersection points where the shape you are copying crosses the grid. This can be done by eye, and the smaller the grid, the more accurate the copy. These are simple curves, and their precise shape is not critical – a 1in (25mm) grid is quite small enough. When you have plotted all the intersections, join them freehand. When joining up the marks on a grid, always keep your hand inside the curve drawn by the pencil. The wristhand and fingers make a good pair of compasses over a fairly limited circumference. Drawing a smooth curve with your hand outside the circumference is more difficult. Cut out the template with a scalpel.

SCREWING AND PEGGING

To conceal a screwed joint successfully, the screw head must be recessed or counterbored below the surface of the wood. Choose a sharp drill a little less than $\frac{3}{8}$in (10mm) diameter (but a fraction larger than the screw head), set the depth stop on the electric drill to about $\frac{3}{8}$in (10mm) and drill the hole down to the stop (Fig. 10).

Fig 10

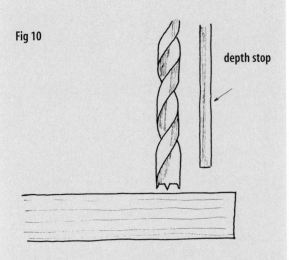

depth stop

Now choose a pilot drill with a diameter slightly less than the shank of the screw (Fig. 11) and drill the pilot hole through the side into the end of the shelf. If you are working in pine or other softwood, the pilot hole for a twin-thread need not reach the full depth of the screw. Drive in the screws and make up plugs or pegs to conceal the screw heads. A plug cutter that fits into an electric drill will make a cross-grained plug, which will hide the hole if fitted carefully (Fig. 12).

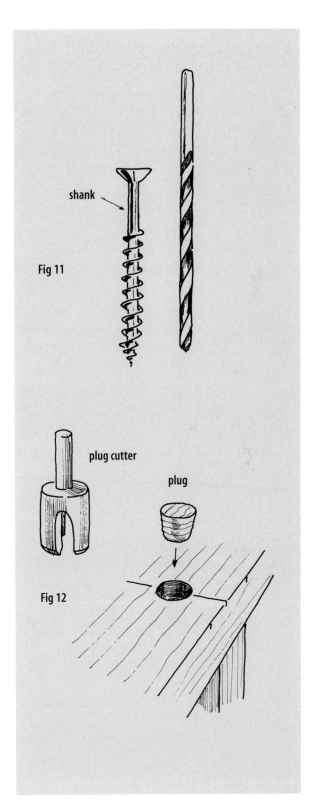

shank

Fig 11

plug cutter

plug

Fig 12

FITTING MIRROR PLATES

You will need two brass mirror plates to hold this rack. The type with the keyhole (Fig. 13) is the easiest.

Position the plates on the back edges of the top shelf, close to the sides of the rack, and prick their location with a knife.

Square across the edge with a set square, and use a cutting gauge to mark in the depth that the plate must be recessed. Use a hacksaw or a dovetail saw to weaken the waste as shown (Fig. 14) and then clamp a board against the shelf to prevent the edges from splitting when the recess is being carved out.

Use a sharp bevel-edge chisel to remove the waste (Fig. 15). Fit the mirror plates, and secure them with countersunk screws.

It is very important that when the rack is fitted to the wall, its sides are vertical and its shelves level. Once you have decided where it is to be placed, mark the position for the anchor screw for one mirror plate, rawl plug the wall and drive in a suitable round-headed screw. Slip the mirror plate over the screw then use a level to determine the exact position of the screwhole for the other plate. With one hole fixed in this way, major inaccuracies are unlikely.

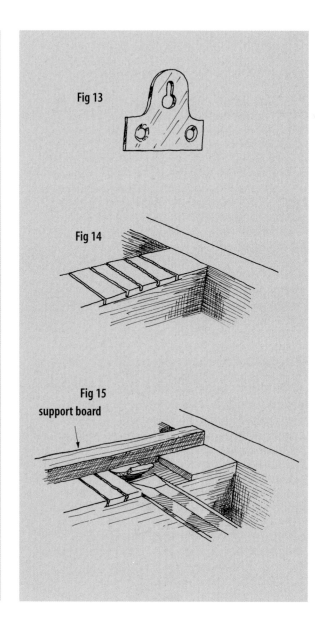

Fig 13

Fig 14

Fig 15
support board

CUTTING LIST

Hanging Rack (nominal sizes: in/mm)

Item	Quantity	Length	Width	Thickness
Sides	2	$27\frac{1}{2}$/699	6/150	1/25
Shelves	2	14/356	6/150	1/25
	1	14/356	5/127	1/25
Frieze	1	14/356	$2\frac{1}{2}$/64	1/25

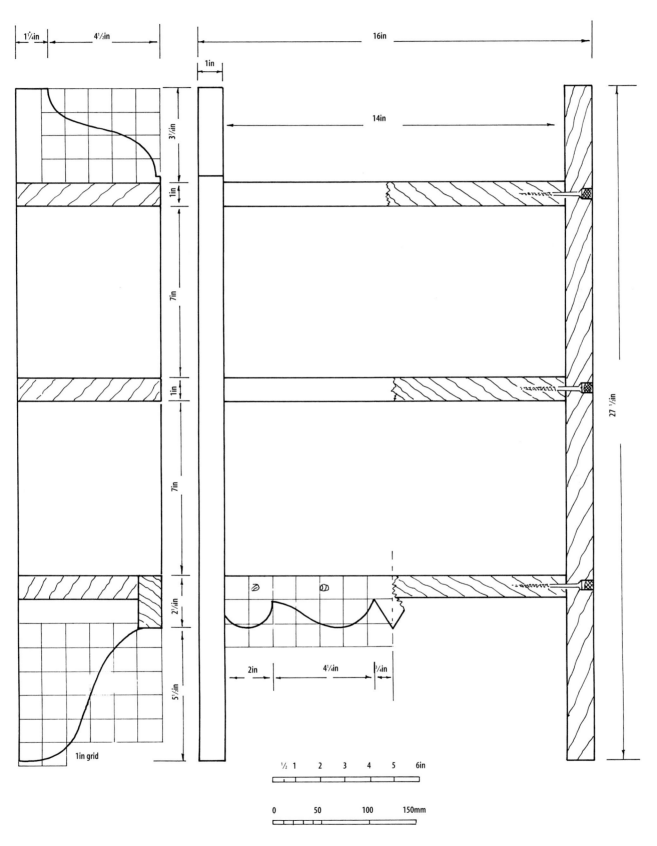

1¹⁄₄in   4¹⁄₈in

1in   16in

14in

3⁷⁄₈in

1in

7in

1in

7in

27¹⁄₈in

2¹⁄₄in

5¹⁄₄in

1in grid

2in   4¹⁄₄in   ³⁄₄in

¹⁄₂ 1   2   3   4   5   6in

0   50   100   150mm

CANDLE BOX

The box featured in the photograph is made from thin planks of yew. The curly grain and fine, smooth, reddish surface is typical of this type of wood. Antique-style candle boxes can be found made from almost any wood. Oak, elm, fruitwood and thin pine are common, but I chose yew because I had a small offcut in the workshop and I was able to saw off enough thin sheets, each a little more than ¼in (6mm) thick, to make the box. I planed them smooth, not without some difficulty because the grain is quite capricious, and then finished with a scraper. They were eventually about ³/₁₆in (5mm) thick.

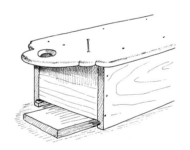

Candle boxes are often dovetailed together, but this one is held with glue blocks and thin nails. Its construction is therefore quick and very straightforward.

METHOD

1 Sort your pieces of wood with some care. The slide must be made from straight-grained and knot-free timber otherwise it might twist or curl after fitting and be difficult to close. The edges of the sides and bottom, which are grooved, should be knot free. It is hard to run a groove through turbulent grain, and short grain would make the fragile edge vulnerable. Cut the pieces to size, plane the surfaces smooth (see Tip, page 36) and the ends square (see Special Skills). Work the groove in the side and bottom planks with a router or scratch stock (Fig. 1).

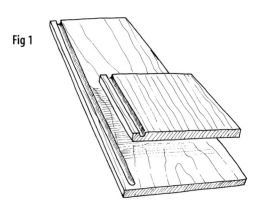

Fig 1

2 Cut a rectangle of fairly thick wood to fit inside the box. This can be left rough sawn, as it is a former around which the box is assembled. Wrap it in cling film to prevent it being accidentally glued in place, and check that it will fit inside the box when the sides and ends are pressed together. They can be held temporarily with rubber bands or masking tape.

  Glue the end to one side of the box, hold the joint together, and wrap it tightly with masking tape. Repeat at the other end, place the former inside, and then glue and tape on the fourth side. Inspect your work to make sure that the back surfaces are level, and that the grooved edges of the sides and bottom are positioned correctly.

3 Pin the joints together and reinforce on the inside with small glue blocks (Fig. 2). Use veneer pins (see Tip, page 159) or panel pins if the wood is over $\frac{5}{16}$in (7mm), and sewing pins (with their heads removed) if it is much less than $\frac{1}{4}$in (6mm). Pin right through the masking tape and tap down the pin heads with a fine nail punch (Fig. 3). Leave the glue to dry.

4 Transfer the curved shape of the candle box back shown on the plan drawing to your piece of wood using the method described on page 28 and cut it out using a fretsaw (see Special Skills). Pinpoint the centre of the $\frac{1}{2}$in (12mm) hole at the top. Unless it is particularly sharp, your drill bit may tear up the edge of the hole. Avoid this by drilling a small

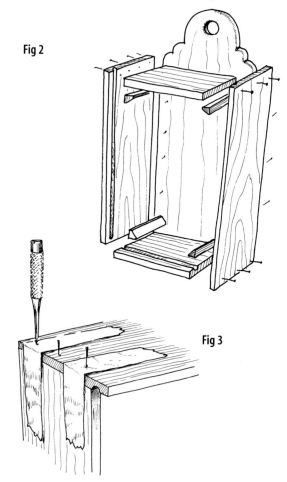

Fig 2

Fig 3

diameter pilot hole in the back board. Then drill a couple of spare boards with the same diameter drill. Sandwich the three together with the back board in the middle, press a nail through all three to line them up, and then clamp them tightly in the vice. Tighten a G-clamp above the nail, and then bore out the hole with a suitable bit.

5   Round all the straightedges of the back board with a shoulder plane and the curved edges with a pen knife (Fig. 4) and sand them smooth (see page 160). While you are still waiting for the glue to dry, cut out and round over the curves at the top of the sliding front, but leave a little excess at the edges for trimming.

Fig 4

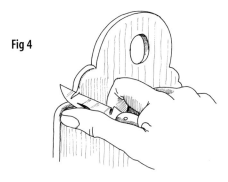

6   When the glue has dried, carefully peel off the masking tape and sandpaper the sides. Place the box onto the back board and remove the former. Using a hard sharp pencil mark around the inside of the box (Fig. 5). This pencil line is your guide for drilling the nail holes through the back board.

Fig 5

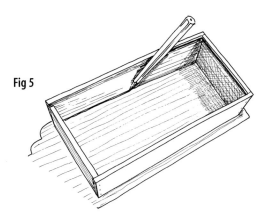

7   Using this line as a guide, drill through the back board using a drill the exact diameter of the pins you will use to hold the box together. If you do not have the right sized drill, wrap a little masking tape around the top of the pin shaft until your drill chuck can grip it. Tighten the chuck, select a low speed and use the pin as a drill (Fig. 6). The hole must go right through, as you will be using this as a pilot hole when you nail from the back into the sides.

Fig 6

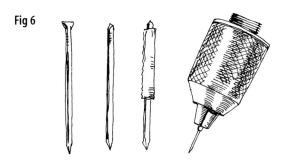

8   Tack a few pins into the pencil line on the back board (Fig. 7). They need not go in far – just enough to locate the box on the back board and prevent it from slipping when you are trying to nail the two together.

Fig 7

Apply glue to the back edges of the box and lower the back board onto them. The pins will hold it in place. Using the pre-drilled holes in the back board, tack the two together, starting with the sides and then the bottom (Fig. 8). Before nailing the top edge, slip some battens beneath the top and the bench to prevent this section of wood being weakened by the hammering.

Fig 8

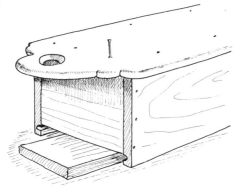

9   Wipe away any excess glue with water and a stiff paintbrush and dry around the joints with an absorbent rag. When dry, trim the front until it fits easily and slides into place.

FINISHING

The candle box featured in the photograph was washed with a coat of dilute tannic acid, dried, sealed in a clear plastic bag and exposed to ammonia fumes. This fuming process is described in more detail on page 86. After quite a short time, the yew loses its reddish-pinkish tinge and turns brown with a hint of green. After removing the box from the ammonia and leaving it to air for a while, I wiped on a coat of English light oak (a Colron stain, available from most DIY stores). The box still looked a little anaemic, so I added a dash of Canadian cedar stain to the light oak.

When this had dried, I applied two rubbed coats of button polish shellac, which left a bright, hard shine. Apply shellac to the inside as well as the outside of the slide. This will stop the slide from warping. After waiting a couple of hours for the shellac to harden, I rubbed down the box with fine 000 wire wool and then waxed it.

TIPS

- When you are planing curly and awkward grain, make sure that your plane is sharp. Move the capping iron right down almost to the tip of the blade and, if the plane is fitted with an adjustable mouth, close it so there is little aperture. Take only fine cuts, lubricate the plane sole with candlewax and plane from any direction that works (Fig. 9).

Fig 9

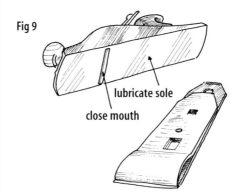

lubricate sole

close mouth

- When you are sanding thin and flimsy structures, place the sandpaper face up on the bench and work the wood across it. For this kind of work 180 grit is quite coarse enough, and 240 is as fine as you will need.

SPECIAL SKILLS

USING A FRETSAW

A fretsaw is an excellent tool for decorative pierced work, marquetry, jigsaw puzzles and for cutting tight curves in thin wood. The saw has a light, sprung frame and screw clamps hold the blade. Different blades are available, from fairly coarse-cutting blades, almost $\frac{1}{16}$in (1mm) thick, to fine thin blades, whose teeth are barely visible. This saw cuts on the downstroke; if you cannot see which way up to clamp the blade, run your finger along it to feel the direction of the teeth.

Workpiece fed into saw by left hand.

Radiating lines indicate centre of support.

Make the saw table to support the work (Fig. 10). Some pencilled lines at the apex of the V will help you to keep the saw in the centre of the small cutting circle. Hold the saw as shown in the photograph (above top), with the handle held vertically and the frame tucked under the right arm. In this position it is clearly impossible to guide the saw around the shapes that are being cut. Instead, the blade is held in one position and gently moved up and down no more than 2in (50mm) in total in a constant and regular motion. Feed the work into the

moving blade with your free hand. This hand also holds the workpiece down on the table and prevents it lifting on the up stroke. The blade is kept moving even when the workpiece is being rotated on the blade to start a cut in a different direction. Once the blade stops it is liable to jam and break.

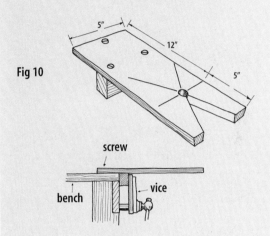

Fig 10

For pierced work, draw the pattern, and drill holes through the wood near the edge of the pattern (Fig. 11). Slip the end of the blade into the hole and tighten the top clamp onto it. Release the blade when that saw cut is finished and move to the next hole.

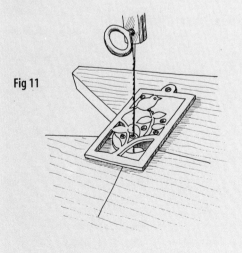

Fig 11

PLANING END GRAIN

Planing end grain is easier if you can use a block plane which has a blade set at an angle of between 13 and 25 degrees to the sole. When the plane blade is set at such a fine angle, the sharpening bevel is on the top of the cutter. Whatever plane you use, make sure that the blade is extremely sharp, its mouth set to the minimum clearance, and the blade set to its finest cut. To reduce noise and blade chatter, ensure that all the screws and clamps holding the blade are tight.

With the plane adjusted correctly, you can avoid the problem of the end of the board splintering by planing the ends before trimming the sides, when you can trim off the resulting split edges (Fig. 12). Alternatively, it is quite easy to plane towards the centre of the board from the edges and, provided you work to a clear line and use a set square, the result should be satisfactory (Fig. 13).

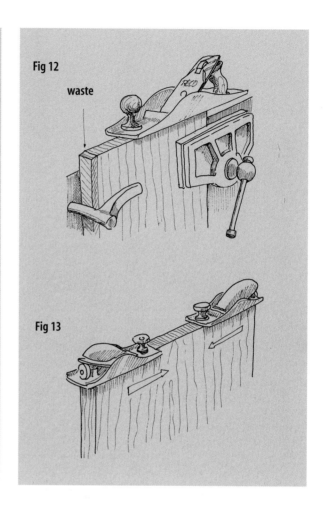

Fig 12

waste

Fig 13

CUTTING LIST

Candle Box (nominal sizes: in/mm)

Item	Quantity	Length	Width	Thickness
Back	1	16/406	$5^3/_8$/137	$^3/_8 - ^1/_4$/10
Sides	2	$12^3/_4$/324	$3^3/_8$/86	$^3/_8 - ^1/_4$/10
Bottom and top	2	$4^3/_4$/120	$3^3/_8$/86	$^3/_8 - ^1/_4$/10
Slide	1	$14^3/_4$/375	$4^5/_8$/117	$^3/_8 - ^1/_4$/10

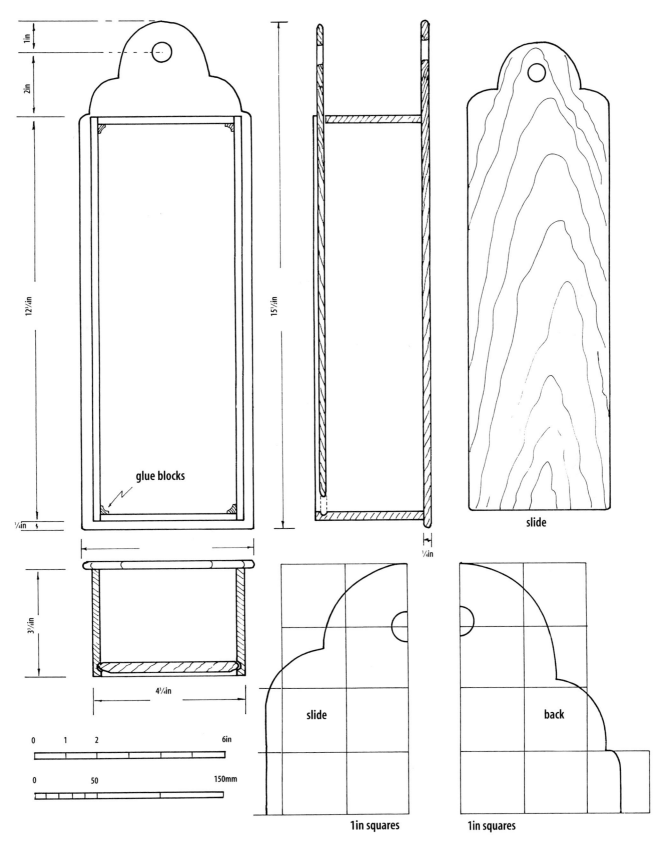

1in

2in

12¼in

15⅛in

¼in

glue blocks

3¾in

4¼in

¼in

slide

| 0 | 1 | 2 | | | 6in |

| 0 | 50 | | 150mm |

slide

back

1in squares

1in squares

JELLY CUPBOARD

This painted cupboard, constructed from planks of the cheapest planed pine bought ready to use from a builder's merchant, is simply assembled. With the exception of its door (which is joined), the cupboard is held together with nails, battens and plenty of glue.

The door, which is mortised and tenoned, has a deep rebate worked in the back, in which the galvanized chicken wire is fastened. If you prefer to make a panelled door you will find instructions on page 133.

This is a kitchen cupboard, useful for storing all kinds of things. Fitted with a perforated zinc mesh, rather than chicken wire, it would have been called a meat safe. The name jelly cupboard

refers to the preserves, jams, marmalades and other home-bottled conserves that can be stored in it. With polished bottles displaying their bright gingham tops and radiant stored fruit, the cupboard looks a picture.

METHOD

1 Choose the planks with care, avoiding any that show cupping or twisting, leaking dribbles of resin, or that do not have a perfect planed surface. The plank from which the door will be cut should be straight grained and as far as possible knot free (see page 20). Leave this to one side. It can be sawn into the appropriate lengths later. Next cut them to length. Measure them accurately, check your measurement, and mark off the right angle on two adjacent faces. Use a handsaw to cut straight down the line. (Sawing need be done only once.) If you take your time there will be no need to trim the sawn edges.

Cut the rebate along the back edge of each side. The quickest and easiest way is to use a plough plane (see pages 151-2). If you are fitting a planked back instead of plywood and need a larger rebate, use the circular saw (see page 69).

2 Join the side planks together, and hold them with battens nailed to the sides on the inside faces (Fig. 1).

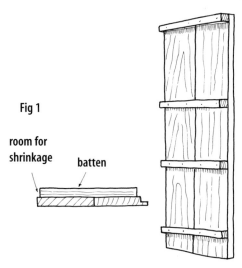

Fig 1

room for
shrinkage   batten

3 Each shelf is made from two lengths of planking. Cut all the shelving to length, and check that it makes up the necessary width. The shelves should be the width of the side planks less the depth of the rebate. Cut two long plywood battens to use as diagonal braces while the bottom shelf is nailed in place. Once the bottom plank is in place, the cupboard can stand upright while the others are slid and nailed into position.

4 Glue and nail the bottom plank at the front onto one side plank. Hold it at right angles to the side and secure it with the temporary batten (Fig. 2). Glue and nail the opposite side, holding it in position with the other batten.

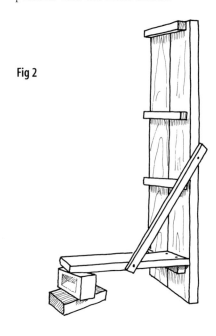

Fig 2

Check that the second bottom plank is exactly the correct width. If it extends beyond the rebate, trim it. Then secure it in place. Now fit all the remaining shelves, press the sides together, and measure the overall width at top and bottom to ensure they are parallel.

5 Nail and glue on the top planks (Fig. 3). Then put the cupboard back on the trestles, front facing up. Saw the two doorframe planks to size, and position them on

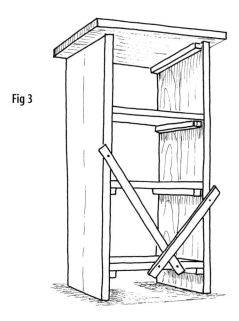

Fig 3

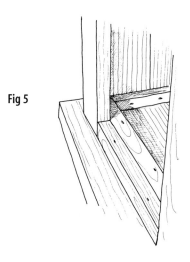

Fig 5

the cupboard. Check that the cupboard is square, then glue and nail on the doorframes. Nail into the side and into the front of the shelves (Fig. 4).

Rest the cupboard on its top, and fasten a batten between the two sides at the top. Fit a second batten to fill the recess formed by the doorframe (Fig. 5).

6   Turn the cupboard on its front, and nail on the back. When the glue has hardened, clean up all the outside surfaces with a plane, and then sand with coarse 60 or 100 grit paper, or a belt sander fitted with a medium grit belt.

Turn the cupboard onto its top, and fit the cavetto (cove or hollow) moulding (see Special Skills) under the top, against the sides and across the front (Fig. 6). Then mark and cut the curves at the bottom of the doorframes and at the sides (Fig. 7).

Fig 4

rough edge   planed edge

overlap   shelf

side

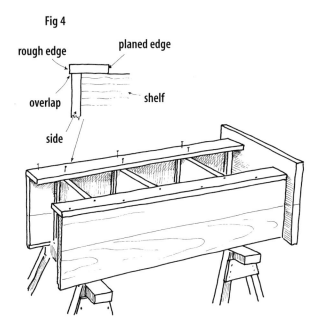

Fig 6

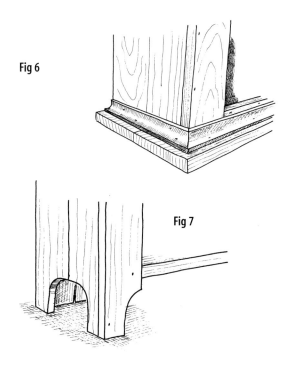

Fig 7

7 Make the door (see Special Skills). When the door has been fitted and hung, remove it, fill all the nail holes, apply knotting to any knots, and then paint the cupboard.

FINISHING

I used oil-based satin finish paints, bought from a local DIY store. One undercoat and two top coats are sufficient, rubbed down lightly in between.

When the paint is dry, fit the wire mesh which can be bought from most DIY stores and garden centres. Do not use second-hand wire, as it will be distorted. Snip the wire to size, lay it gently in the rebate, and hold it there with short pins driven against the wire mesh. Bend the pins over the wire and tap them in tight to secure it.

Fit long battens into the rebate to conceal the edges of the chicken wire, nailing them with veneer pins.

SPECIAL SKILLS

CUTTING AND FITTING THE CAVETTO MOULDING

This standard moulding, normally available in hardwood and softwood, can be bought ready machined from your DIY store or builder's merchant.

The moulding at the corners is mitred at 45 degrees. Having cut the first mitre, hold the moulding in place, and mark off the position for the other end (Fig. 8).

Draw in the mitre line and saw it using a cutting jig. Position it and then cut the sides (returns) a little longer than is strictly necessary to allow for adjustment. Tack the two returns in position with panel pins, and gently plane the faulty mitre until it fits. Use a shoulder plane, and work slowly and carefully, moving the tool with your thumb and

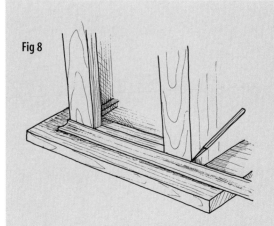

Fig 8

fingers rather than your arms (Fig. 9). A little wax on the sole of the plane will make this easier. For adjusting the angle of a planed edge see page 122.

Glue and nail the front strip first, and then remove the side strips one at a time, and fasten them.

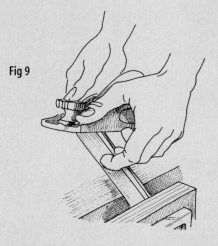

Fig 9

MAKING THE DOOR

1 Plane the door members, then mark the face edge and side. Put the stiles in place in the doorframe, and mark off the front shoulders for the rails, and the position of the rails on the stiles (Fig. 10).

Square around the shoulder line at each end of the rails, using a knife at the front face, and a pencil elsewhere. Put the two stiles together and transfer the marks across. At the inside edge of each end of the stiles will be marks showing the position of the rails. These lines do not define the extent of the mortise.

Fig 10

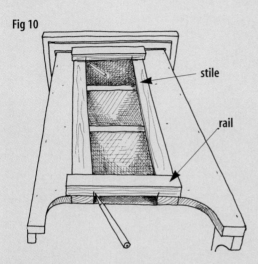

stile

rail

2 Now mark in the mortise at each end of the stiles. They should be ¼in (6mm) wide and stop ¾in (19mm) from the end of the stile (Fig. 11). Cut out the mortises (see page 65). Then using the same mortise gauge setting, mark in the tenons around the ends of the rails (Fig. 12).

Fig 11

¼in

¾ in

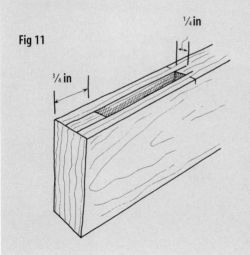

Fig 12

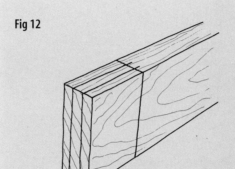

3 Cut out the rebate at the back of each piece. You will find that the rebate removes or just grazes the inside edge of the mortise. Evidently, the tenon shoulder on the inside will have to be longer than the one at the front to fill the rebate (Fig. 13). Mark this long shoulder in pencil, and when you cut it, cut on the waste side to allow a little for adjustment (Fig. 14). Next saw the sides of the tenon, but do not cut beyond the shoulder lines (Fig. 15).

Fig 13

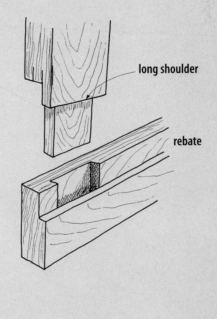

long shoulder

rebate

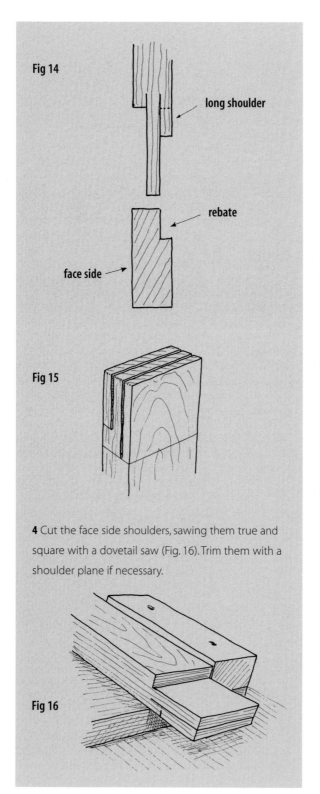

Fig 14

long shoulder

rebate

face side

Fig 15

4 Cut the face side shoulders, sawing them true and square with a dovetail saw (Fig. 16). Trim them with a shoulder plane if necessary.

Fig 16

5 Cut the inside long shoulder (Fig. 17) and then cut out the small haunch in the outside edge of the tenon, using a tenon saw and splitting out the waste with a bevel-edge chisel. Trim the shoulder square with the front shoulder (Fig. 18).

Fig 17

Fig 18

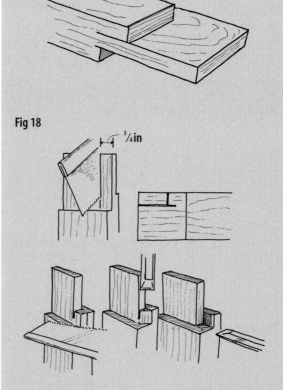

¾ in

6 Press the tenon into the mortise. With a little adjustment you should find the joint fits well. If the shoulder on the front face doesn't meet the stile, trim away the long shoulder. If the long shoulder doesn't meet but the short one does, leave things as they are – the short shoulder on the showing face is the important one (Fig. 19).

Fig 19

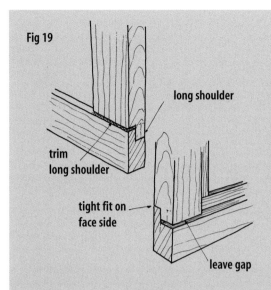

long shoulder

trim
long shoulder

tight fit on
face side

leave gap

7 Cut the other tenons and fit them. Then check and correct the door for any twisting. Using through tenons reduces the chance of any twist being built in to the door by badly cut mortises, but small amounts of wind can be corrected by shaving away the tenon or loosening the mortise. It is preferable not to have to do this, as it weakens the joints. Remember that the door is pressed against the shelves when it is shut, and since it is a fragile door, it will probably lie quite flat.

HANGING THE DOOR

You will need eight ¾in (19mm) countersunk screws to hold the hinges. In addition it is helpful to have perhaps four ½in (12mm) screws of the same gauge with which to position the door. You will need a sharp bradawl, and a suitable screwdriver (one that fits the screw head slot and is the same width). Trim the door to fit. Lift the cupboard onto its back and put the door in place. Mark in the locations for the three hinges. Mark in pencil on the door and its frame the top and bottom marks for each hinge (Fig. 20), ensuring they line up.

Fig 20

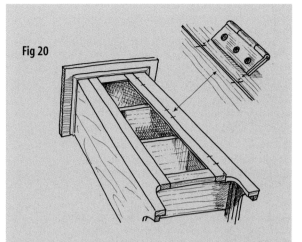

Set the cutting gauge as illustrated (Fig. 21). Remove the door and square off the end marks of the hinge on the door and on the frame. Saw down the end marks and make a few relieving cuts between them to weaken the wood (Fig. 22).

Fig 21

Fig 22

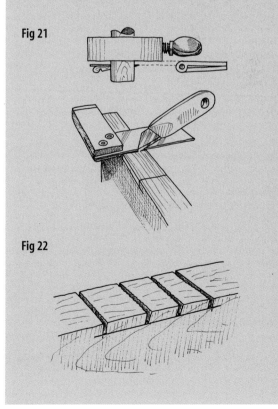

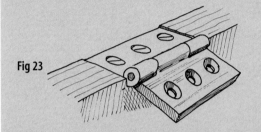

Remove the waste with a bevel-edge chisel.

Screw the hinges to the door, positioning them as illustrated (Fig. 23). Then lift the door into place. The closed hinges should slide into their slots in the doorframe. Adjust the ends of the slots where necessary but do not deepen them. If the door seems too wide with the hinges in place, it may be necessary later to trim back the outer edge of the door.

Fig 23

Remove the door, open the hinges, and clamp a plank of wood to the bottom of the door that will hold it steady while the hinges are screwed to the frame. Position the hinges in the frame, as illustrated

(Fig. 24). Put in a temporary, ½ in (12mm), screw at the top and bottom hinges, pulling them up tight, and check to see how the door closes. The door should be flush with the frame when it is shut. Some adjustment can be obtained with the second and third screw in each hinge. When you are happy that it is properly in place, put in the remaining screws. If you had to remove screws in the fitting, use the bradawl to bore a deeper hole, and use a slightly longer replacement screw.

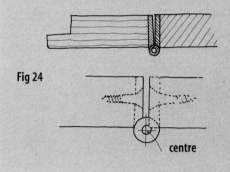

Fig 24

centre

CUTTING LIST
Jelly Cupboard (nominal sizes: in/mm)

Item	Quantity	Length	Width	Thickness
Top	2	26/660	6/150	1/25
Top	1	26/660	3½/89	1/25
Sides	4	45/1145	6/150	1/25
Front	2	45/1145	5/127	1/25 Offcuts for battens
Shelves	6	21½/546	6/150	1/25
Door				
Stiles	2	41/1040	3/75	1/25
Rails	2	16/406	3/75	1/25

Back, tongue and groove to make panel: 45 x 22 x ⅝in (1145 x 558 x 16mm)

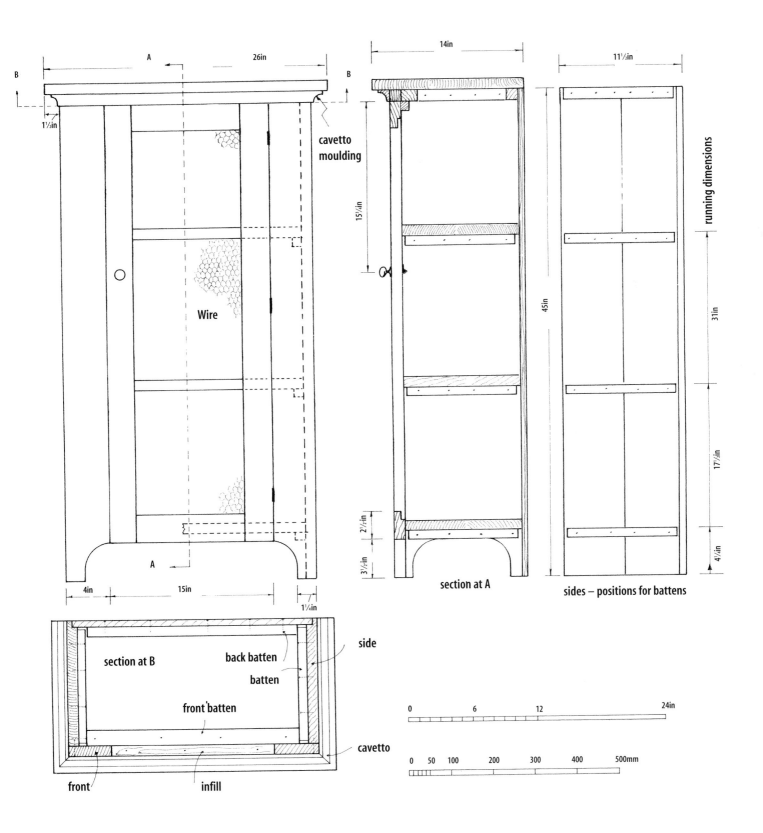

B

A ← 26in →

B

1½in

cavetto
moulding

Wire

A →

4in

15in

1¼in

14in

15½in

45in

section at A

2½in

3½in

11⅛in

running dimensions

31in

17¾in

4¼in

sides – positions for battens

section at B

back batten

batten

front batten

side

cavetto

front

infill

0   6   12   24in

0   50 100   200   300   400   500mm

49

FIVE-PLANK
STOOLS

There are several stools illustrated in the photograph. One is made from yew, the Gothic-style stool is fumed oak, the box stool is made from unstained oak, and the painted stools are pine.

Antique examples of these stools can be found dating from the late fifteenth century, although most date from 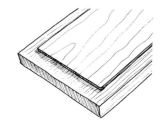 the late eighteenth century. In antique footstools, the plank feet are tenoned into the top with two small through tenons at each end. I have described how to nail the stool together rather than join it, but it is a simple matter to tenon the legs into the top. Instructions for cutting mortise and tenons are on page 147. If you intend to tenon the legs, remember when marking out to lengthen the leg planks by the thickness of the top.

With the exceptions of the box and the Gothic stool, all the pieces shown here are nailed together. The nails are punched in with the holes left unfilled except where the stool has  been painted. The oak stools are fastened with glue and wooden pegs, but when they were made, I held them with twin-thread woodscrews, which I removed after the glue had dried.

METHOD

PAINTED SQUARE STOOL

1   Cut out the components. The width of the top plank will probably determine the width of the stool. Cut the legs so that they are slightly narrower than the top plus the thickness of two side planks, as illustrated (Fig. 1).

Fig 1

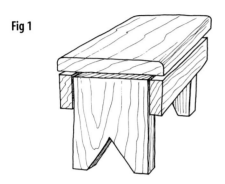

2   Hold one leg in the vice, position one end of the top over it, and glue and nail them together. Repeat at the other end.

3   Glue and then clamp a side plank into position (Fig. 2). Nail it into the sides of the legs, first making sure that the legs are vertical. Leave the clamp in place until the glue has dried.

Fig 2

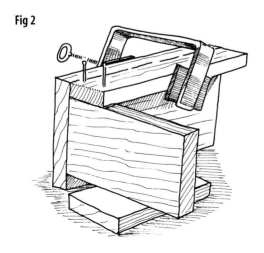

Fit the other side plank in the same way. Saw the V in the ends with a cross-cut saw. Then mark off and saw the S in the top with a jigsaw, having first drilled a pilot hole in which to start the blade.

4   Plane the edge of the top plank flush with the side planks, and radius the top edges of the stool (Fig. 3). Lastly, punch down the nail heads, fill the holes using two-part wood filler. and sand the stool.

Fig 3

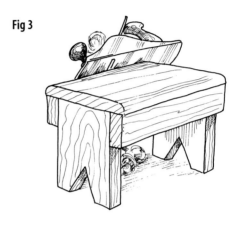

FINISHING

The slightly transparent paint finish of the stool featured in the photograph is easy to achieve, and easy to adapt if you want a similar effect using different colours.

After filling the nail holes and sanding the filler smooth, wash the stool over with a fairly weak solution of blue aniline dye. This is a quick-drying stain, soluble in methylated spirits. (Suppliers of aniline stains, and the dry earth colours mentioned below are listed at the back of the book.)

When it was dry, I mixed some burnt sienna earth colour with water, adding PVA glue and stirring it to make a thin, watery paint, which I brushed on quickly and thinly.

The water in the paint raised the grain of the pine, producing a rough surface. I left it to dry then sanded the stool with 180 grit paper and waxed it.

YEW AND PAINTED PINE STOOLS

You will notice in the plans that the top of these stools is the same width as the top of the legs, and the side planks clamp against the top, rather than support it.

1   Make a paper template for the frieze and one of the legs. Saw out the top and the two legs. When sawing the legs, saw the angle at the top of each one at the same time.

　　If they are marked as illustrated, one angled saw cut will cut the ends of both legs (Fig. 4). Finish shaping the legs, and plane the sides smooth and square.

Fig 4

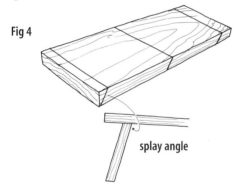

splay angle

2   Mark the position of each leg across the underside of the top. Hold one leg in place, its angled end flat against the top, and run a pencil along the inner and outer edge (Fig. 5). You will then have two lines defining the joint at the top of the leg. Tack panel pins along the lines to guide the leg back into place.

Fig 5

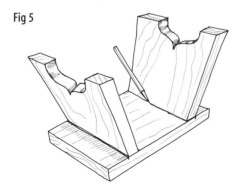

With the top still inverted, drill a series of pilot holes for the nails through the top. Hold the drill at the angle at which the legs splay, otherwise the nails will break out (Fig. 6).

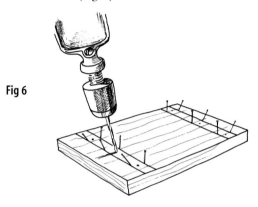

Fig 6

3   Hold one leg plank tightly in the vice, apply glue to its top edge, and lower the top plank over it. Nail through from the top to secure it (Fig. 7). Repeat at the other end.

Fig 7

Put the top and both legs in the vice as shown, and plane the sides of the legs and the edges of the top flush (Fig. 8).

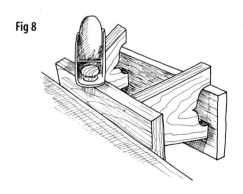

Fig 8

4   Glue the side planks to the edges of the top, and nail and glue them to the legs (Fig. 9). When the glue has dried, plane the radius at the top edge. Mark and cut out the frieze, fill the nail holes and sand the stool smooth.

Fig 9

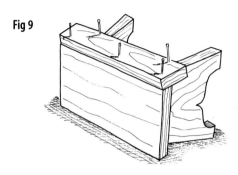

FINISHING

The yew stool is just waxed, the pine stool has been painted with a thin blue paint, made by mixing blue and green dry colours with a quantity of burnt sienna dry colour, water and PVA. It was then quite vigorously sanded using 100 grit paper, rubbed in the direction of the grain, to cut through to the wood, giving a slightly distressed, used appearance.

OAK GOTHIC STOOL

1   Cut out the top, the legs and the side planks. When you cut the side planks to width, leave them slightly oversize so that they can be trimmed to fit later.

Work the moulding in the top, and cut the slots and shapes in the legs (Fig. 10). Mark the notches with a pencil, but incise them with a knife before cutting. Cut on the waste side of the line, and the saw should leave a clean cut.

Fig 10

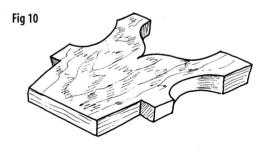

Sand all the flat surfaces smooth, but do not round off the edges of the legs or side planks.

2   Screw and glue the top to the legs. If you are using twin-thread screws which you are going to remove later, there is no need to bother to counterbore or countersink them, just drill the thin pilot hole.

3   Plane the top edges of the side planks so that they can be slid tightly into position against the underside of the top plank and against the notches in the legs. Once they are fitted, mark the positions of the legs and saw off the waste at the ends (Fig. 11).

Fig 11

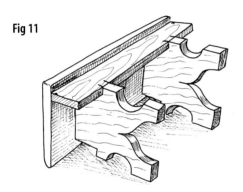

4   Cut out the frieze on both side planks (Fig. 12), glue them in position, and hold them with short twin-thread screws. When dry, remove each screw, one at a time, and bore the screw holes out with a ¼in (6mm) drill. Carve wooden pegs to fit the holes. Put a little glue in each hole, and drive in the pegs, trimming them flush with a saw and chisel.

Fig. 12 shows the frieze cut leaving some

Fig 12

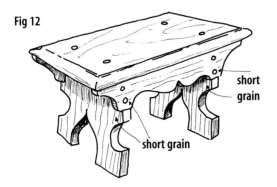

short grain

short grain

vulnerable short grain, which might split or break. If it weren't a copy of a sixteenth-century stool, you might be excused for thinking it wouldn't last.

FINISHING

This stool has a fumed finish. Oak naturally turns dark when exposed to ammonia fumes. After masking off some areas of the stool with tomato ketchup (see page 86) I tied it in a bag with a dish of ammonia, leaving it until the stool had darkened.

After washing off the ketchup and allowing the stool to dry, I rubbed it down with 240 grit paper and waxed it with a slow-drying brown wax polish. I followed with a vigorous application of hard, quick-drying black wax, and burnished it with a lambswool buffer attached to an electric drill.

OAK BOX STOOL

This is a six-plank stool which was the most fun to make. My oak planks were too thick, so to begin with I used the adze and handsaw on the inside faces until they were about the right thickness. Only the underside of the top (which I sawed) was reasonably flat. The other pieces were left scalloped and undulating.

1   Cut the ends and sides to size. Hold them together to see how they fit. You may need to level the ends of the sides with a rebate plane so that they lie flat against the ends.

If you do, mark them with a pencil as illustrated (Fig. 13), strike off a thickness line with the gauge and cut down the pencil line to the thickness line with a tenon saw. Remove the waste with the rebate plane (Fig. 14).

Hold the sides together again, keeping them in position with some rubber bands. It is likely that the joint between the sides, ends and bottom will have lots of gaps in it unless the lower part of the sides are levelled with the rebate plane.

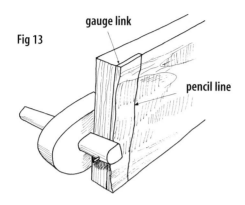

Fig 13

gauge link

pencil line

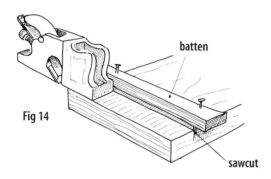

batten

Fig 14

sawcut

2 Mark off and level with a chisel the position on each leg where it joins the bottom plank (Fig. 15).

Fig 15

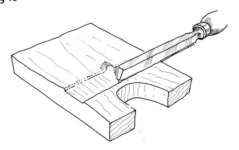

3 Glue and screw the top sides to one end leg. Trim the bottom plank until it fits between them and then glue and screw the other leg in place (Fig. 16). This, too, will need some adjustment.

Drive a couple of screws through the sides into the bottom to help hold it.

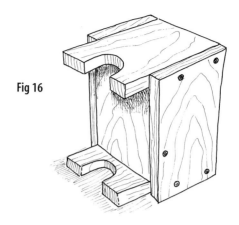

Fig 16

4 When the glue has hardened, trim the sides of the stool flush with the ends. Remove the screws and replace them with oak pegs, then use a V-parting chisel to define the edges of the moulding on the top, finishing off the moulding with a small gouge (Fig. 17).

Fig 17

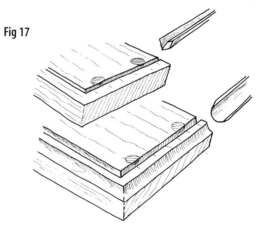

Fit the top using small T-hinges, readily available from your local ironmongers. Screw them to the top, and then mark and cut the slots for them in the top edge of the back plank (see page 47) and screw them in place. Fit the hook, and the nail it locates against in the front of the box.

This box stool was left unfinished. It looks good now, and will look even better with age.

SPECIAL SKILL

CUTTING A ROUNDED EDGE MOULDING

Mark the moulding freehand with a pencil. By holding the pencil quite loosely, and allowing your other fingers to trail along the edge of the board, you will draw a fairly accurate parallel line. Go over the line with a cutting gauge set to the same distance. Set a plough plane, router or rebate plane to a $\frac{1}{16}$in (1mm) depth of cut, and form the rebate around the edge of the top.

Using a rebate plane, start with the sides and take off the corners in easy stages. Continue working around the top of the stool, including the ends, removing the corners to produce a slightly elliptical curve. Work on the underside of the top too, to lighten its appearance.

When the moulding is almost finished, file or grind a flat scrap of metal into a crude scraper, leaving the burrs on the edge of the tool. Hold it in one hand and draw it around the edges to remove the remaining corners and unify the appearance of the work. Finish with sandpaper wrapped around a shaped block.

CUTTING LIST

Stools (nominal sizes: in/mm)

Item	Quantity	Length	Width	Thickness
Painted Square Stool				
Top	1	11/280	8/200	1/25
Legs	2	7$\frac{1}{2}$/190	7/178	1/25
Sides	2	11/280	3/75	1/25
Yew and Painted Pine Stools				
Top	1	12/305	6/150	1/25
Legs	2	7$\frac{1}{2}$/190	7/178	1/25
Sides	2	12/305	3/75	1/25
Gothic Stool				
Top	1	14$\frac{1}{4}$/362	7/178	$\frac{3}{4}$/19
Legs	2	6$\frac{3}{8}$/162	7/178	$\frac{3}{4}$/19
Sides	2	14$\frac{1}{4}$/362	3/75	$\frac{3}{4}$/19
Oak Box Stool				
Top	1	13$\frac{3}{8}$/340	8/200	1$\frac{1}{4}$/32
Legs	2	8$\frac{3}{8}$/213	6/150	1$\frac{1}{4}$/32
Sides	2	12$\frac{5}{8}$/320	6/150	1$\frac{1}{4}$/32
Bottom	1	10$\frac{1}{4}$/260	6/150	1$\frac{1}{4}$/32

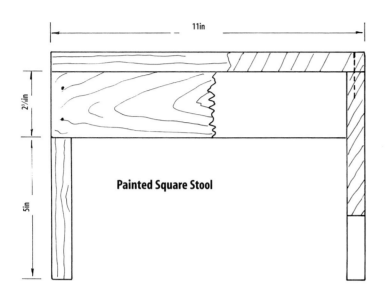

Painted Square Stool

11in

2¹⁄₄in

5in

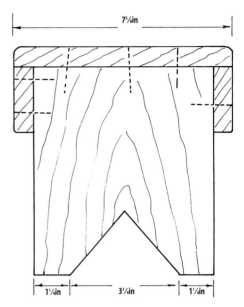

7⁵⁄₈in

1¹⁄₄in   3³⁄₄in   1¹⁄₄in

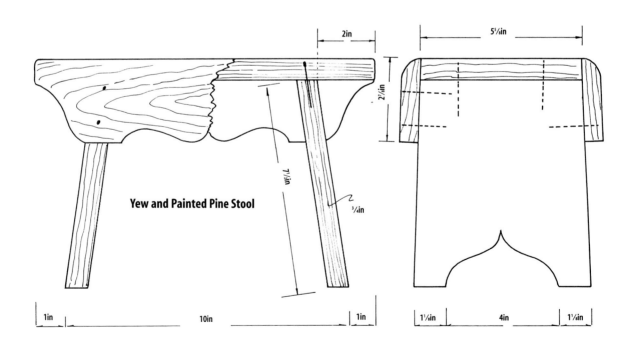

Yew and Painted Pine Stool

2in

2⁷⁄₈in

7¹⁄₄in

³⁄₄in

5⁵⁄₈in

1in   10in   1in

1¹⁄₄in   4in   1¹⁄₄in

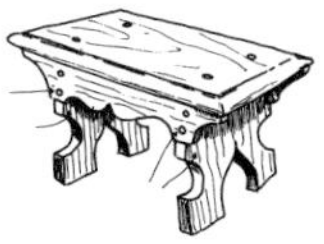

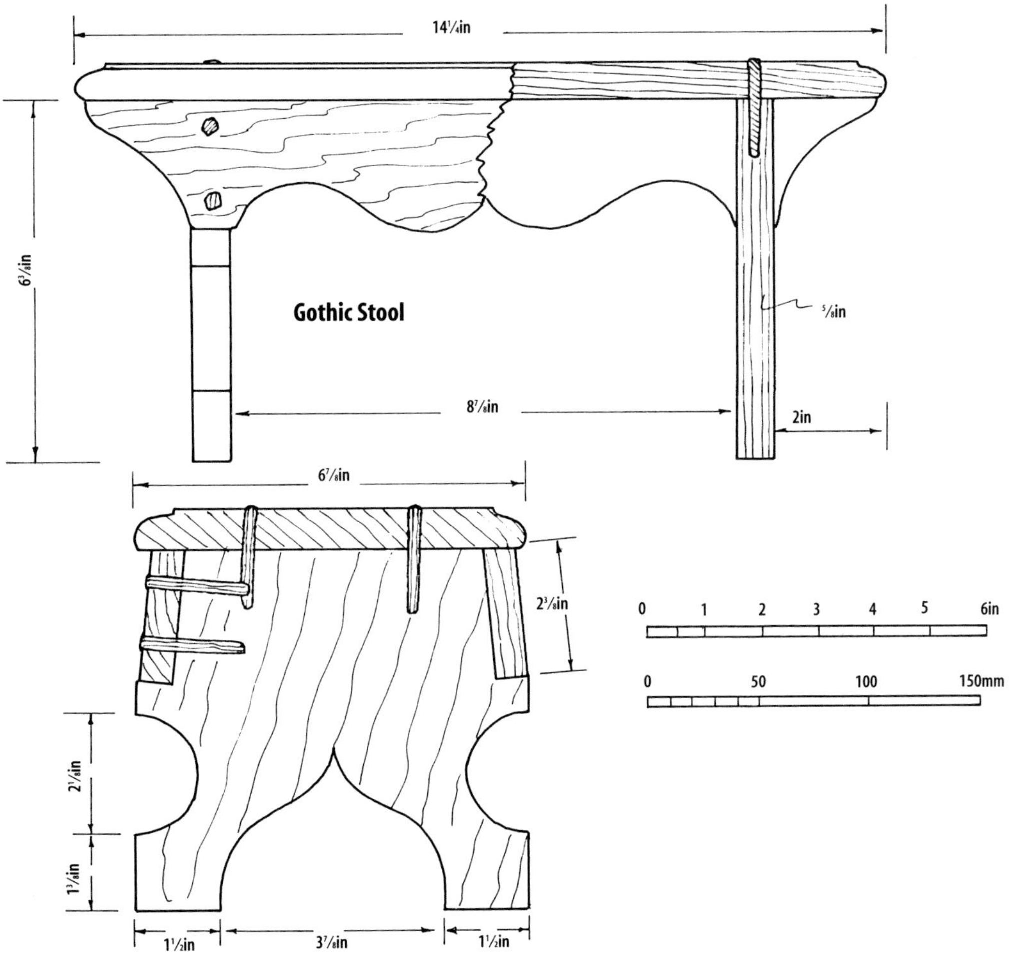
14¼in
6⅜in
Gothic Stool
⅝in
8⅞in
2in
6⅞in
2⅜in
2⅛in
1⅜in
1½in
3⅞in
1½in
0
1
2
3
4
5
6in
0
50
100
150mm

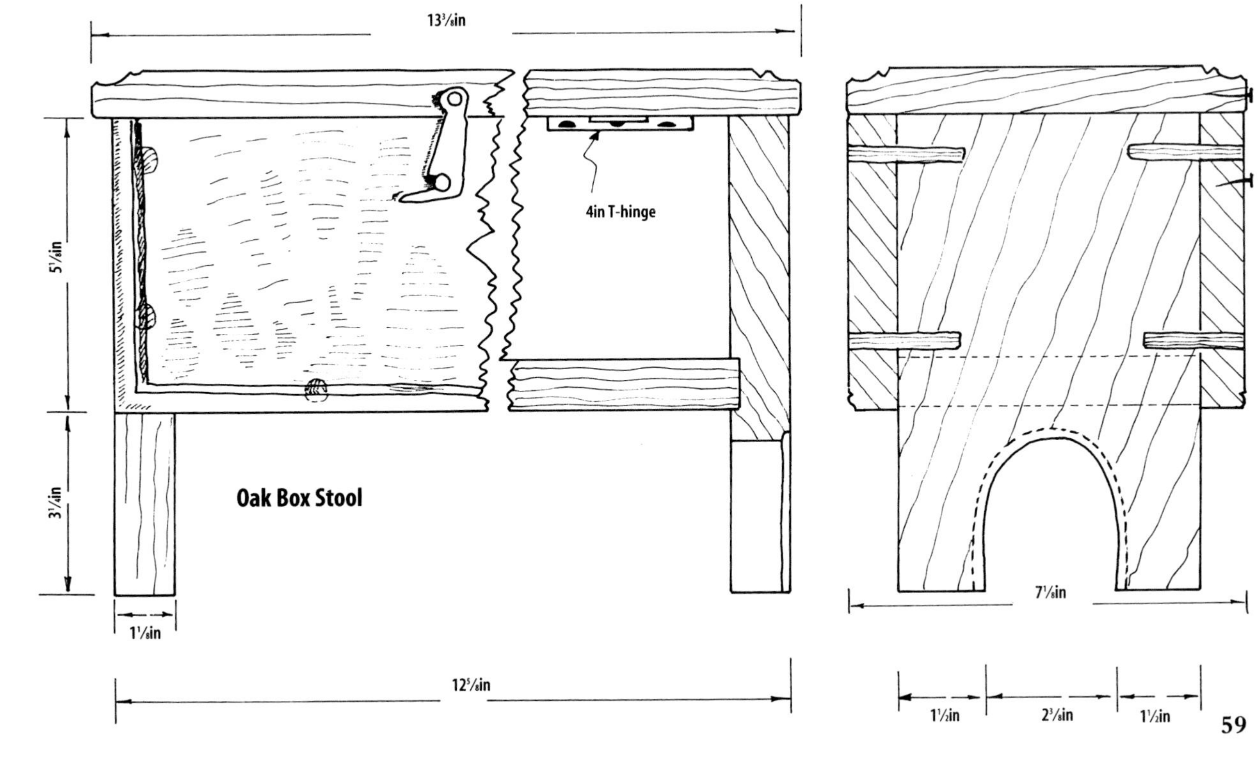
13⅜in
5⅛in
4in T-hinge
3¼in
Oak Box Stool
1⅛in
12⅝in
7⅛in
1½in
2⅜in
1½in

KNEEHOLE DESK

This kneehole desk is a copy of a small and dilapidated nineteenth-century pine desk found hidden away at the back of a bric-à-brac store in Frome, Somerset. It was finished with black bitumen paint, its fastenings were rusty, and the hand-carved wooden knobs replaced earlier brass

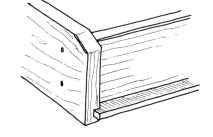

handles. Despite the damp and neglect, the structure was more or less intact. If the desk had been oak, the nails would have rotted away long ago and restoration would have taken a lot longer.

It is made simply from pine boards. The only joints are in the panel framing at the back, the other components being glued and nailed together. It is, however, essential that the marking out of the drawer runners, and the

sawing of the different components is accurate.

I used galvanized wire nails in most places but chose aluminium lost heads to hold the drawer runners to the thin sides of the pedestals, where the strength of the join is in the glue. They do not hold as well as galvanized nails, but the sides are thin, and where the points poked through I was able to sand them flat with the belt sander.

METHOD

1 Select your wood and cut each piece exactly to length. Choose the best planks for the top to minimize shrinkage (if possible, use planks cut from the centre of the log or cut on the quarter). In addition, use better quality boards for the outside faces of the pedestals, and for the panels, outside pediment moulding and drawer fronts. Use the inferior boards for the drawer sides and backs, inside pediment moulding and drawer runners.

Use a circular saw to cut the battens that hold the top together and the drawer runners that hold the pedestal sides together.

2 Assemble the top, and mark on it the positions of the four battens. Glue the top together (see page 42), clamp it and secure it with the battens nailed and glued in position.

3 Cut out the planks that will make up the two pairs of pedestal sides. Treat them as pairs – it is essential that the drawer runners of each pair are in line, or the drawers will be difficult to fit.

Assemble one pair of pedestal sides, front edges together and ends all aligned. Mark off the positions for the drawer rails and square across the full width of the pedestals (Fig. 1).

Fig 1

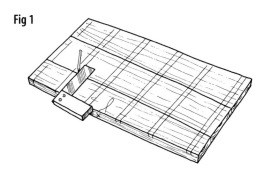

Glue the sides together and clamp them with a pair of sash clamps while you nail on the runners. Join up the second set of sides.

4 When it is dry, plane off any excess glue and, if necessary, run the plane along the top edge of the pedestals. If there are any major misalignments at the top, make the correction on both of the pair. Slight misalignments at the bottom of the sides will be hidden by the pediment and will not matter.

Put all four pediment sides together to check they are the same width, adjusting the back edge until they are.

5 Lay the top, face down, on a pair of trestles, and tack to it a temporary batten in place of the panel frame. This will help you line up the pedestal sides and makes it easy to fasten a diagonal supporting batten while you are erecting them (Fig. 2).

Fig 2

Glue and nail the outer sides of the pedestal to the top and support them with diagonal battens (Fig. 3).

Fig 3

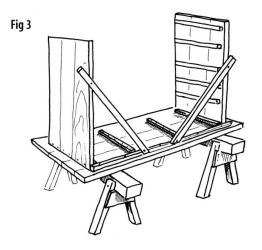

6 Hold one inner side in place, checking that its face is parallel with the other sides when sighted down the fronts. Do not trim any wood from the front top corners of the sides, because this will lift all the drawer rails on that side. If a side leans back compared to the outer side, fit a little wedge at the back to bring it level. If it leans forward, you can safely trim the back corner until it is true (Fig. 4).

Fig 4

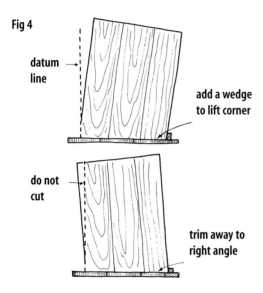

datum line

add a wedge to lift corner

do not cut

trim away to right angle

Glue and nail the side, and then fit and fasten the remaining side (see page 42).

Each pair of sides should be parallel. Adjust the inner sides until they are parallel with the outer, then hold them in position with braces.

7 Make up the panelled framework (see Special Skills). Remove the braces holding the sides, and the temporary batten tacked to the underside of the top, and fit the panelled framework in position. Before fastening it, identify two or three nail hole positions in the top by drilling them through from the underside (Fig. 5), and then glue and nail the framework to the ends of the pedestal sides. Turn over the desk and nail down through the top into the top framework rail.

Fig 5

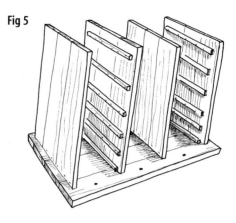

8 Cut all the drawer rails. Their exact width will probably vary slightly according to the position of the drawer runners, but if you make them a little wider than necessary, they can be planed flush with the front once they are fastened in place (Fig. 6).

Fig 6

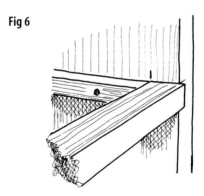

Fix the rails level with the tops of the drawer runners. A simple clamping technique will accomplish this. Fit the rails from the top down, nailing the topmost rail into the underside of the top. Nail in the remaining rails from the sides (Fig. 7).

When the glue has dried, plane the front edges of the rails flush with the sides.

9 Fit glue blocks to the underside of the top and the sides of the pedestal to support the arch over the kneehole, and then fit a board neatly into the space (Fig. 8). Cut it to shape and glue in place.

Fig 7

Fig 8

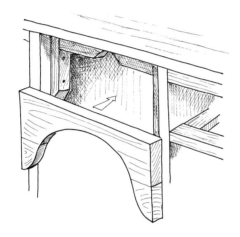

Fig 9

Fig 10

11 Fit a doubling-up piece beneath the bottom drawer rail on each side to support the front sections of skirting (Fig. 11). Then fit and nail the skirting to the outside of each pedestal, finishing flush with the front and back edges.

10 Make up the skirting. This is just a straight bevel planed on the upper corner of the pediment. Do not plane the bevel on the section of pediment that is at the back of the kneehole.

Before fitting the pediment, place the desk on the floor and mark in pencil the top height of the pediment, all around the desk. Fit the unbevelled section of pediment first, cutting it to length, and nailing and gluing it against the lower panel framework (Fig. 9).

Fit the two 'returns' on the inside of the kneehole. They should finish flush at the front edge (Fig. 10).

Fig 11

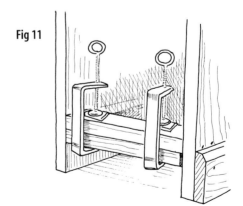

Fit the skirting across the front of the pedestals, and across the back, nailing and gluing it in place. When dry, trim as illustrated (Fig. 12).

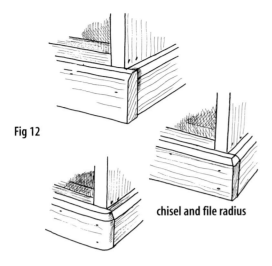

Fig 12

chisel and file radius

12 Make the drawers (see Special Skills). Sand the desk all over in preparation for finishing.

FINISHING

When the depressions caused by the nails had been filled and the desk sanded smooth, it was painted over with a coat of Venetian red powdered pigment dissolved in a small quantity of water. PVA glue, which was used as the binder, left a rough finish, so the surface was again sanded smooth. Two more coats of paint were needed to achieve an even finish, which coloured the wood but did not obliterate the grain markings. Some additional touching in with a thin brush and a thicker paint mix was necessary to conceal the filler.

After sanding, the surfaces were fixed with a coat of button polish, and then the lines were painted, using a mixture of flake white and ochre dry pigments, mixed with water and PVA adhesive to make a thick cream consistency. A good quality watercolour brush steadied against a straightedge gave a satisfactory line on the top, sides and panelling. The lining around the drawers was carried out freehand to save time.

Two final coats of button polish were applied, rubbed down with wire wool and followed with one coat of brown wax.

TIPS

• Apply PVA glue just before the joint is ready for assembly. If you spread the glue too soon, the wood fibres will absorb the moisture and swell, making the joint difficult to press together.

• Fit the deepest drawers first. If you make a mistake it will probably fit one of the shallower drawers higher up.

SPECIAL SKILLS

MAKING A FRAMED PANEL

For the framework you need fairly knot-free wood. If the wood has knots, try to position them where they will not weaken the mortises and tenons or interfere with the grooves.

Cut the framework members to length. Plane them square, and mark the face edges and face sides.

Clamp the two stiles and two muntings together with their ends aligned. The stiles are mortised at the ends, and the muntings are tenoned into the framework rails, but the shoulder lines for all eight joints are identical. Mark them with a knife (Fig. 13). Note that the tenons at the ends of the rails are stub tenons, which do not pass right through the stiles, so the mortises in the stiles are marked on the inside (joining) face only.

Put the two stiles in their correct positions relative to each other, and mark off the shoulders of the two rails. Square round all the shoulder lines for the tenons (ends of the top and bottom rails, ends of the muntings).

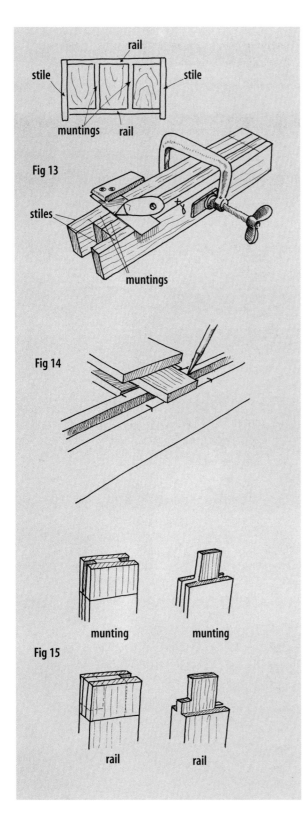

Fig 13

rail

stile

stile

muntings

rail

stiles

muntings

Fig 14

Fig 15

munting

munting

rail

rail

Clamp the two rails together (shoulder lines aligned) and mark in the positions of the four mortises for the muntings. Lay out the framework roughly with face sides showing. Number the joints. Mark on each member the position for the grooves to hold the panel. The muntings each have two grooves, one each side (Fig. 14).

Position the ¼in (6mm) groove in the centre of the wood. Notice that the grooves will reduce the width of each tenon by the groove's depth (Fig. 15).

Cutting the Joints

Cut the tenons first. Set the mortise gauge to the width of the ¼in (6mm) mortising chisel. Mark and saw off the waste areas above the haunch, and the two sides of the groove that will go to waste when then tenon is cut (Fig. 16) and mark the tenons with a gauge (Fig. 17), then saw down the sides of the tenons with a handsaw. Remove the waste with a tenon or dovetail saw.

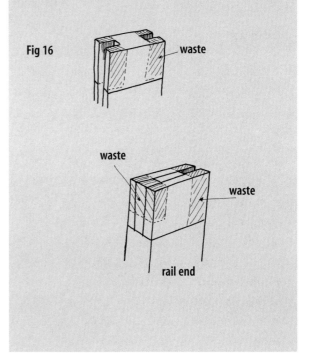

Fig 16

waste

waste

waste

rail end

Fig 17

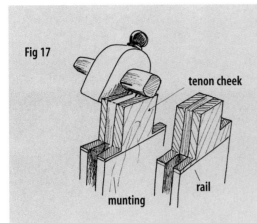

tenon cheek

rail

munting

The tenons at the end of the top rail are reduced in width at the outer edge (Fig. 18), and the remaining heel of the tenon, known as the haunch, nicely fills the groove.

Fig 18

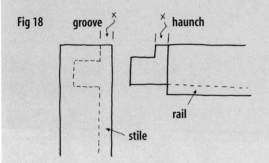

groove

haunch

rail

stile

Taking one joint at a time, place the tenon in position across the mortise and line up the shoulder marks. Pencil in the length of the mortises. Cut out the mortises and fit the tenons as you go. Check the tenons for straightness or 'wind' and shave away the tight side of the mortises with a chisel where necessary.

Make up the width of the panels and glue them together (see page 42). When they are dry, cut the panels to their exact size. This is found by assembling the framework, taping it together with masking tape, and measuring it. Check the diagonals of the frame

before measuring the width and height of the recesses with a pair of straight, thin battens poked into the grooves.

Make allowance for shrinkage and swelling when you are cutting out the panel. Movement along the grain is going to be slight, and the panels should be $1/8$in (2mm) shorter than the overall distance between the grooves.

Movement across the grain is considerable, however, and the allowances you make will depend on the moisture content of the wood you are using. If you are working in hot summer weather and the air is dry, you can reckon that the panel will swell later in the year when the weather turns damp and cold. Settle for $3/8$in (10mm) less than the overall width. If the weather is cold and damp when you are making the desk, the panel is likely to dry out and shrink when it is brought indoors, so settle for a panel $3/16$in (5mm) less than the overall width.

Plane the front face of the panel smooth and flat, and then reduce the width at the edge by planing a wide bevel on the inside face.

Before you assemble the framework with its panels, check that the panel sits easily in the grooves. The fit can be assessed by drawing an offcut trimmed from the end of a stile (with a sample of the groove worked in it) along the edge of the panel. This is called mulletting and you must not forget to do it.

Assemble the framework. Set up all the components of the framework where they can be easily recognized. Squirt glue into the bottom rail mortises and slip the muntings in place (Fig. 19). Fit the middle panel between the muntings, and glue and slip the top rail in position. Tap it down, check that the joints are tight, then insert the two remaining panels (Fig. 20) and glue the stiles into position. Knock all the joints together. A panel pin driven into each tightly closed joint will help to hold the frame while the glue hardens.

Fig 19

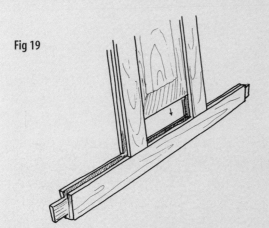

Fig 20

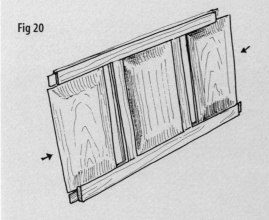

MAKING DRAWERS

The illustration shows the construction details of the drawer (Fig. 21). Notice that the sides, which are lapped to the front, conceal the groove worked in the drawer front. Do not make the groove too deep.

Cut out the drawer fronts, and number each one after it has been fitted. With some slight variation, all the drawer fronts will be the same length. The

drawers are wider at the bottom, and you should fit them first (see Tip, page 65).

Fig 21

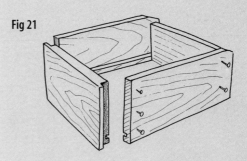

Take one front at a time. Adjust its height until each end can be slid into position. Then trim the ends to fit.

When all the fronts are cut, fit the sides. Again, trim the heights first and then the ends. Make the drawers about 1in (25mm) shorter than the runners. It will make it easier to fit the drawer stops if they are all a regular length. Once they are trimmed, leave them in position on the drawer runners.

Groove the sides and front to fit a ¼in (6mm) plywood bottom board.

Cut the lap joints in the ends of each drawer front.

Cut and fit the back boards. These will be the same length as the distance between the laps on the front. The illustration shows how the back sits on top of the plywood base, with its top edge lower than the sides (Fig. 22).

Fig 22

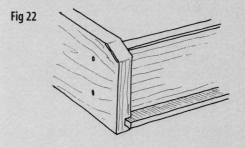

Cut out the drawer bottoms. They are plywood and should be a tight sliding fit. Cut all the boards slightly oversize and trim them to fit the individual drawers.

Glue and nail the drawers together. Assembly will be easier if the bottom is fitted in position once the front and one side are nailed together. Punch the nail heads slightly below the surface of the sides, and, once the bottom is firmly in place, pin the bottom board to the back of the drawer.

Fit the drawers. They may need trimming before they slide smoothly, not because the sides are too wide but because the runners are not perfectly level. It is sometimes necessary, therefore, to trim one side rather more than the other.

When all the drawers fit, cut and glue in place the bearing strips that broaden the bearing surfaces of the drawer and help hold the plywood. These can be held in place with weights while the glue dries, but there are so many drawers that it is easier to hold them with a few small veneer pins. If they are punched below the level of the bearing surfaces they will not score the runners (Fig. 23).

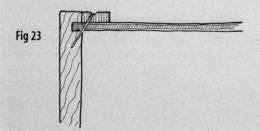

Fig 23

Drawer stops are fitted last. These take the shock of the drawer when it is slammed shut. Fit the ones at the top drawer first, and glue and pin them to the rail. Position them with the end grain towards the approaching drawer. In place, they should keep the drawer front just flush with the edges and rails of the pedestal.

Cutting a Lap Joint for a Drawer

Trim the joining edges straight and square. Then set a cutting gauge to the depth of the lap (Fig. 24).

Fig 24

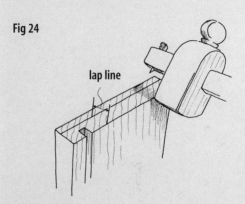

lap line

Set the circular saw fence to the thickness of the side plank (this dimension includes the thickness of the blade), and set the height of the blade to the depth setting of the cutting gauge. If you can, set the angle fence to right angles, so that it will hold and control the drawer front. Check your saw settings with a test piece and adjust if necessary.

Before making the saw cut, use the cutting gauge to incise the lap line. This is a precaution; if any of the short grain weakened by the saw cut is inclined to flake off, it will tend to break at the line and will not mess up the joint.

Cut the depth cut, then remove the drawer front and place it edge up in the vice. Remove the waste with a wide sharp chisel, lodging it in the gauge line, and knocking it with a mallet. If necessary, clean up the lap with a rebate plane.

To assemble the joint, hold the drawer front in the vice, with the lap facing the bench. Spread glue in the rebate forming the lap and position the side carefully. Press it tightly against the drawer front using a sash clamp and nail it in place.

1in grid

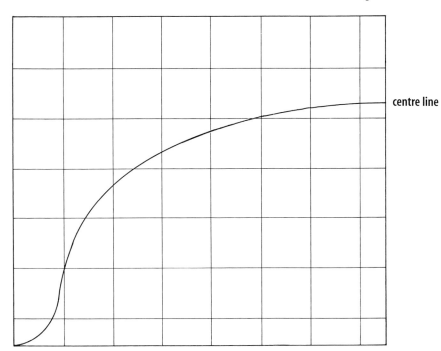

centre line

Pattern for arch over kneehole

CUTTING LIST
Kneehole Desk (nominal sizes: in/mm)

Item	Quantity	Length	Width	Thickness
Top	4	39$\frac{1}{2}$/1003	6/150	$\frac{3}{4}$/19 Excess for runners
Sides	12	30/760	6/150	$\frac{3}{4}$/19
Drawer rails	6	14/356	6/150	$\frac{3}{4}$/19 Excess for runners/battens
Framework rails	2	37/940	3/75	1/25
Stiles and munting	4	30/760	3/75	1/25
Panels	4	24/610	6/150	$\frac{3}{4}$/19
	2	24/610	7/178	$\frac{3}{4}$/19
Pediment moulding	4	18/457	6/150	$\frac{3}{4}$/19 Excess for runners/battens
	3	15/380	6/150	$\frac{3}{4}$/19 Excess for runners/battens
	1	39/990	6/150	$\frac{3}{4}$/19 Excess for runners/battens
Drawers				
Front	10	10/255	6/150	$\frac{3}{4}$/19
Sides	20	15/380	6/150	$\frac{3}{4}$/19
Back	10	9/230	6/150	$\frac{3}{4}$/19
Bottoms	10	15/380	9/230	$\frac{1}{4}$/6 Plywood
Arch	1	15$\frac{1}{2}$/395	5/127	1/25 Use offcuts to complete

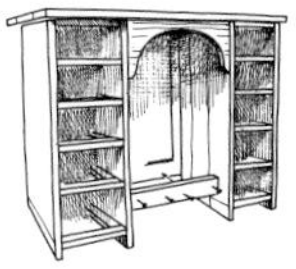

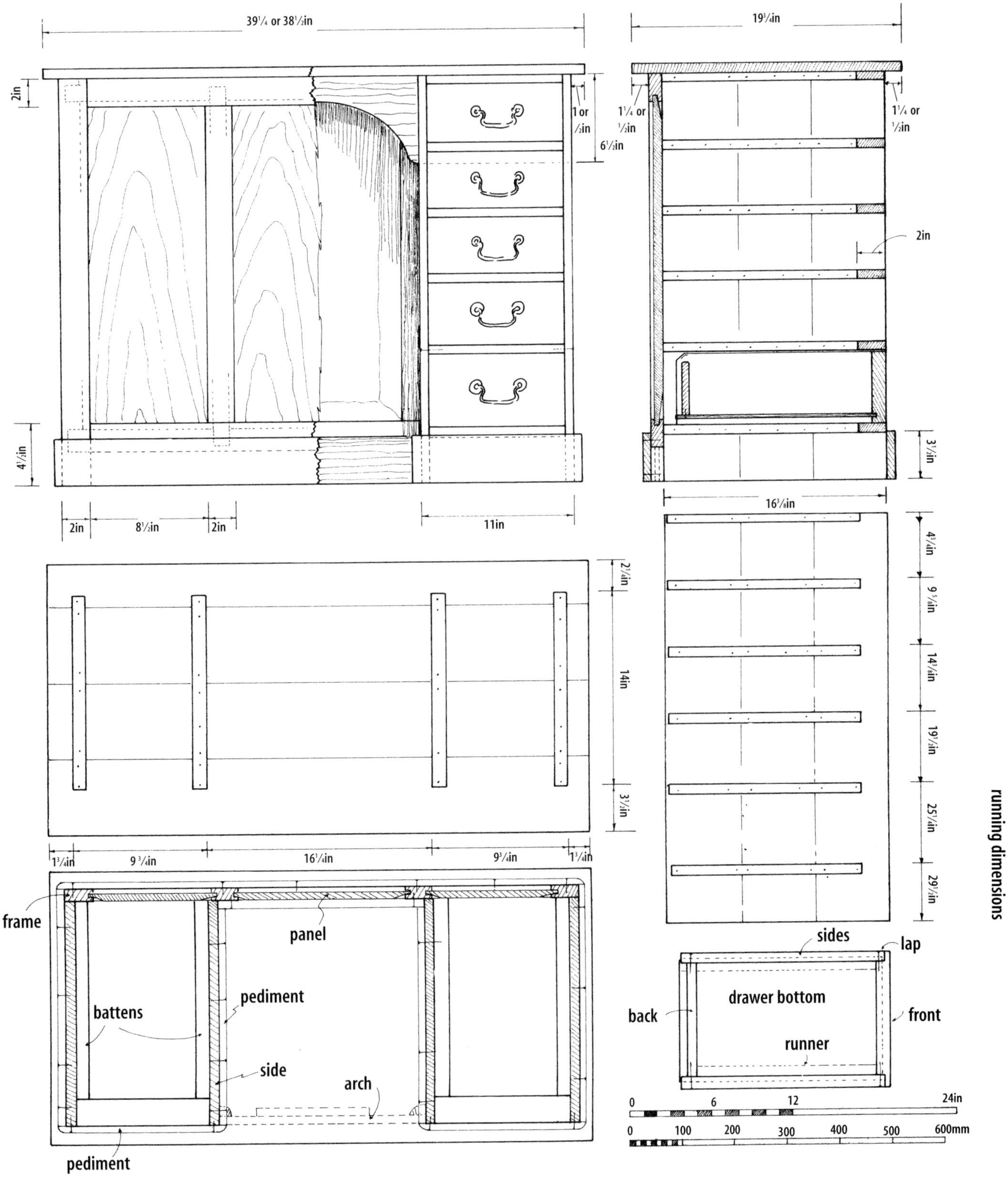
39¼ or 38½in
19¾in
2in
1 or ½in
6½in
1¼ or ½in
1¼ or ½in
2in
4½in
3½in
2in
8½in
2in
11in
16⅜in
2¼in
14in
3¼in
4¾in
9⅝in
14⅜in
19½in
25¼in
29½in
running dimensions
1¾in
9¾in
16¼in
9¾in
1¾in
frame
panel
pediment
battens
side
arch
pediment
sides
lap
back
drawer bottom
front
runner
0
6
12
24in
0
100
200
300
400
500
600mm

CHILD'S CHAIR

This is a copy of a child's chair that was made in about 1840. It is made from ash, a strong, springy wood, regularly used for chair making. It is relatively knot free and easy to carve with a knife. The chair can be made from virtually any wood, but if you are going to use the techniques I suggest, choose a straight-grained, knot-free plank. Unseasoned wood is much easier to work with the tools I recommend (and it is cheaper). You will need a piece about 1¼in (32mm) thick.

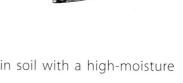

Before it was painted, the ash of the back legs was darker and browner than that of the rails and back splats, even though the pieces were all cut from the same log. This tingeing, known as black heart or brown heart, is thought to occur when trees grow in soil with a high-moisture content. Although the discoloration is not associated with weakness, affected planks are usually sold at a discount by timber merchants.

This style of this chair is typical of home-made chairs of the nineteenth-century American Midwest. The tops of the back legs are curved and flattened on the front faces into 'rabbit ears' or 'donkey ears', and the seat is formed from a single sheet of rawhide, wrapped around the stretchers while wet and pulled tight with laces underneath.

METHOD

There are some special tools used in making this chair, including a side axe. Penknives are easy to come by, although I prefer not to use a heavy, fat, multi-purpose penknife for whittling. A simple two-bladed knife, of the kind produced by Taylors, IXL or Eye Witness of Sheffield, is ideal. They have good quality blades, which can be honed to a razor edge, and smooth, comfortable handles.

Rusty drawknives can be found in many junk shops, but they are not often worth buying. Marples make a heavy duty drawknife, and the Woodcraft catalogue shows not only a carver's drawknife and a light and slightly cranked German drawknife, but also an American carpenter's knife. It is not essential to use these tools – chisels and planes will do – but the job will take longer.

1   Make a template of the side elevation of the back leg from cardboard. Mark out the back legs using the template, then the front legs, rails and stretchers. You can cut all three back slats from a single, 1¼in (32mm) thick plank. Use a jigsaw to cut out the back legs.

The remaining pieces are straight and can be cut with a circular saw. The front legs of the chair should be sawn 1¼in (32mm) square; the rails and stretchers should be slightly less than 1in (25mm) square.

2   Fit the brace with the ⅝in (16mm) drill bit and bore through a small offcut. This hole will guide you when you carve the ends of the stretchers, which should be ⅝in (16mm) in diameter.

Shape the rails and stretchers first. Use the axe to remove the corners and, as you become familiar with using the axe, begin the shaping. This is quite a roughly hewn chair, and irregularities do not matter. Once you have roughly shaped them, put the pieces on the shaving block and clamp them

securely with a G-clamp (Fig. 1). Use the drawknife to remove the corners and bring them down to a regular size. It is dangerous to use the knife if the workpiece is insecure.

Fig 1

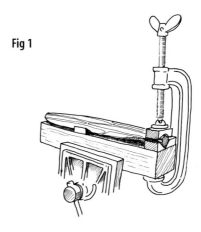

With a little practice, the drawknife gives a perfectly acceptable finish, but if you want to improve it still further, trim the workpiece with a plane. I used a shoulder plane, holding the end of the stick in one hand and propping the other end against the bench hook, and took fine shavings (Fig. 2).

Fig 2

3   By now the stick should be almost the right size. Try pushing an end through the sample hole you bored earlier. Shave it until it slips in to a depth of about ¾in (19mm).

Finish all the rails and stretchers except for the front one, which needs a little embellishment. Take the stick for this stretcher and mark the centre and ends of a lozenge-shaped bead (Fig. 3). Use the axe to reduce the stick to a cylinder and taper the ends of the stretcher with the drawknife, trimming them to ⅝in (16mm) in diameter to match the others.

Then, with a penknife, gently carve the shoulders of the lozenge (Fig. 4). Work the remaining curves in a similar way.

Fig 3

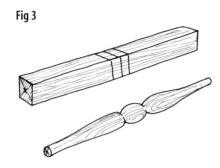

Fig 4

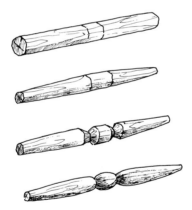

4   The front legs are reduced in diameter between the arm rests and the seat stretchers. Mark them out while the wood is still square, identifying end marks and the new, smaller diameter (Fig. 5). Use a jigsaw or a coping saw to cut away the waste (Fig. 6).

Trim the front legs to a straight cylinder, 1¼in (32mm) in diameter, and then round off the shoulders and the smaller diameter section in between with a penknife.

Fig 5

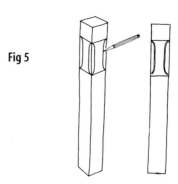

Fig 6

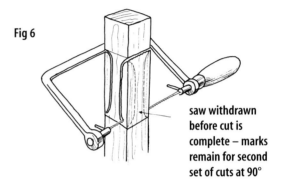

saw withdrawn before cut is complete – marks remain for second set of cuts at 90°

5   Start shaping the back legs. The illustration shows the different sections of the back leg at different heights (Fig. 7). For the most part, the back legs are a regular oval section.

Fig 7

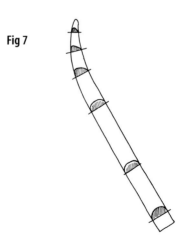

Clamp both legs together in the vice and plane the curved rabbit ears, which start just above the seat stretchers (Fig. 8). Trim off the corners, and

round off the back edges, taking care to work with the grain (from the top downwards) when shaping behind the ears.

Fig 8

Round off the lower front section of each leg, and finish off with a shoulder plane or spokeshave.

6   Sand these components to remove splinters and any hard or sharp edges. Begin with 100 grit sandpaper and finish with a soft foam backing block, working in the direction of the grain.

7   Cut out and smooth the back slats. At this stage they are sawn and planed flat; they will be bent later. Plane a radius on the top edge of each slat.

Take the template for the back legs and mark on it the exact position and size of each back slat mortise. Then mark and clearly label the positions for the back rail and stretcher, the armrest, rail and stretcher, and the front ones. A single template will be enough, as long as the marks are clear (Fig. 9).

Fig 9

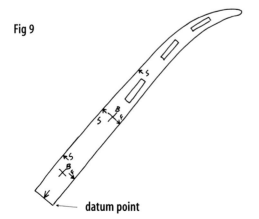

datum point

8   Support the leg and chop out the mortises for the back slats with a mallet and ¼in (6mm) mortise chisel (Fig. 10). They should be ½in (12mm) deep and angled slightly towards the back to accommodate the slightly bowed back slats (Fig. 11).

Fig 10

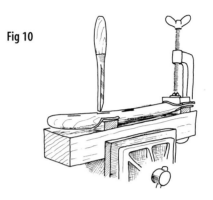

Fig 11

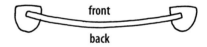

front

back

9   To bend the back slats, make the simple former illustrated in Fig. 12. Because there is always a certain amount of spring-back after the wood has been released from the former, the curve is slightly exaggerated. Place the slats between strips of plywood to protect them from damage by the clamp and blocks.

Fig 12

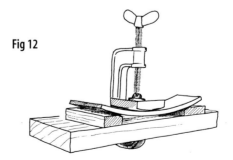

Put the three slats in a deep roasting tin and pour boiling water over them. Leave them to soak for about 20 minutes. Try to maintain the water temperature either by heating the tin or by replenishing it with fresh hot water. Remove them from the tin, stack them together and clamp them to the former. Leave them for a day.

10 Take the pair of back legs and mark the centre lines for the rails and stretchers on both planes. From above, the sides of the chair are seen to be slightly splayed, so the holes for the side members will be drilled at a point a little past the 90 degree mark (Fig. 13). Use the template to mark the centre points for each hole.

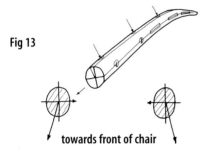

Fig 13

towards front of chair

I recommend that you bore the holes with a brace and bit rather than with an electric drill. It is important that the auger bit is sharp. Drill the holes in the back legs for the rail and seat stretcher. After shaping the top corners of the top slat, fit the slats and stretchers into the back legs. Trim them to fit and then drip a little glue around and in each hole and mortise before knocking them in quite hard. Correct any twist in the assembly before tightening with a tourniquet (Fig. 14).

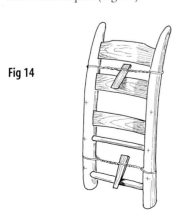

Fig 14

11 Drill the holes in the front pair of legs for the rail and stretcher. Assemble them, check that the legs are parallel, then glue them together, holding them with a tourniquet.

When the tourniquets are released, drill the holes for the side rails and stretchers, remembering that when they are seen from above, the front legs are farther apart than those at the back, so the holes you drill will have to be at the appropriate angle (Fig. 15). Use a jig to hold the legs at the correct angles, while they are drilled (see page 96).

Fig 15

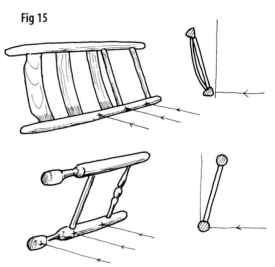

Angles at which holes should be drilled to house rails and stretchers.

12 Assemble the chair, and if everything fits, glue it together.

FINISHING

This chair was undercoated with a pink oil-based priming paint. It was sanded when dry and a home-mixed paint, made with powdered rose pink dry colour with a little burnt turkey umber, some PVA glue to bind it and water, was applied. The simple lining was first painted freehand with bright yellow acrylic paint and then overpainted with a Humbrol gold paint.

CHILD'S CHAIR

SEATING

The seating material was a small sheet of rawhide, which arrived in a brittle roll that was soaked in the bath for about an hour.

While the hide was softening, I made a brown paper template of the seat, including a wrap of 3in (75mm) at each stretcher (Fig. 16). The softened rawhide was laid on newspaper and the outline of the template was marked on it and then cut out with heavy-duty scissors.

Fig 16

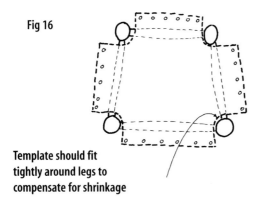

Template should fit tightly around legs to compensate for shrinkage

I punched holes around the edges of the leather and cut some thin rawhide thongs to lace the underside. The seat was then placed over the stretchers and laced up. Where necessary, the laces were joined with a sheet bend (Fig. 17). The rawhide shrinks and hardens as it dries, leaving the seat drum tight.

Fig 17

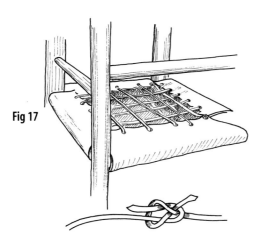

TIP

To control the depth of a cut when drilling, simply bore a sample hole in an offcut. Before drilling, stick a slip of masking tape to the side of the bit at the correct depth setting. From the moment the screw thread bites into the wood, count the number of revolutions it takes to reach the mark. From then on, when you are drilling the chair holes, just count the turns.

Controlling the direction of the hole is also surprisingly easy. Fig. 18 shows a simple jig that will allow you to sight the direction and hold the assembled back or front legs at the correct angle (assuming the drill is held and worked parallel to the bench top). The drill is lined up with the lines drawn on the board. The legs are clamped at the correct angle, so you need only keep the drill in line with the marks and parallel to the bench. You can even guarantee that the bit remains parallel by tacking a strip at the edge of the bench the exact thickness to prop the bit, and keep it level, as shown in Fig. 19.

Fig 18

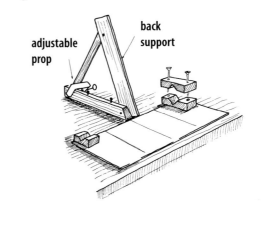

adjustable prop **back support**

78

Fig 19

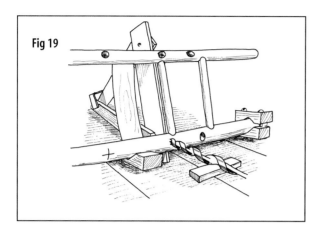

SPECIAL SKILLS

USING A SIDE AXE, DRAWKNIFE AND PENKNIFE

All these tools must be very sharp indeed. They should be able to slice a fine shaving with a slow, gentle stroke.

Side Axe

You will need a cutting block resting on the floor to absorb the energy of a side axe. Don't use the bench – you will be surprised at how much damage can be done by a few careless slashes.

Hold the workpiece with one hand well above the axe head. Never lift the blade to the same level as your hand unless you are trimming a wide piece of board and your hand is well out of the way.

Use short gentle cuts, dropping the blade no more than 3–4in (75–100mm). The axe head should slip down the piece you are working, with its bevel on the outer edge. Once you have started a shaving, continue slicing it down to the cutting block. When you are starting a fine shaving it sometimes helps to drop your wrist. This alters the cutting edge to an acute angle, making it easier to control the cut.

Drawknife

You need both hands to control this tool, so the work must be securely anchored. A vice or a G-clamp will do, but for rounded work you must use a notched pad beneath the clamp to increase its grip. Flimsy wood, like the rails and stretchers of the chairs featured here, must be supported along their length. The simple arrangements illustrated in Fig. 10 are quite adequate.

Grip a handle with each hand, the tool resting on the workpiece with the sharpening bevel upwards. The depth of cut is increased by dropping the handles slightly. You will find that you can remove ¼in (6mm) thick shavings quite easily. Draw the tool towards you. If you come to a knot, you can use the tool in the reverse direction, but in general it is easier to control if you draw it towards you.

Penknife

Compared with most other tools the penknife has a tiny blade, and it doesn't take long to make it razor sharp. Hold the handle and workpiece in your right hand, and lodge your left thumb against the back of the blade. With both hands holding the workpiece you can impart considerable cutting power by pressing the blade into the wood with your left thumb.

USING A SPOKESHAVE

Spokeshaves are held with both hands, and can smooth quite tight curves. As with a drawknife, they are generally pulled towards the operator. The wooden spokeshave with the tanged blade is more difficult to control than the all-metal spokeshave, particularly when the wooden mouth is worn, but it is more versatile, slipping into tighter curves than its metal counterpart.

If you are using a wooden spokeshave, hold it with your wrists up, and index fingers gripping the blade directly below the tangs. This helps keep the blade from dragging out. Once you have sharpened the blade of a metal spokeshave, adjust its setting, test it and then screw up the cap iron really tight to prevent the blade moving or chattering.

MORTISING A CHAIR BACK BY HAND

You will need a ¼in (6mm) mortising chisel and a mallet. If you only have one chair to mortise, it is quicker to do it by chisel than to use a router and not at all difficult.

Having marked out the mortise in pencil, incise around the edge with a knife. Start ⅛in (2mm) from the top end and make your first cross-grain cut (Fig. 20). Move the chisel along an ⅛in (2mm) and make the next cut, and so on until you reach the end. After the first cut, subsequent cuts will each loosen a chip, leaving a trench about ⅛in (2mm) deep (Fig. 21). Once the first row is finished, clean away the loose chips and begin a second row, hitting the chisel a little harder. Three times down the length of the mortise should be enough to reach ¾in (19mm).

Clean out the mortise, check it is the right depth and trim the ends square with a chisel.

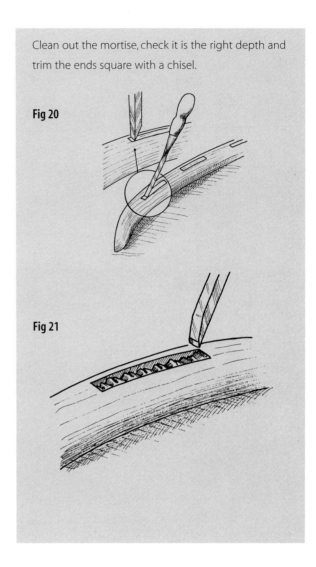

Fig 20

Fig 21

CUTTING LIST
Child's Chair (nominal sizes: in/mm)

Item	Quantity	Length	Width	Thickness
Front legs	2	16¾/425	1¼/32	1¼/32
Back legs	2	27½/699	2¾/70	1¼/32
Stretchers	4	12/305	¾/19	¾/19
Rails	3	12/305	¾/19	¾/19
Arm rests	2	12/305	¾/19	¾/19
Front rail	1	12/305	1/25	1/25
Back slats	3	10/255	3/75	¼/6

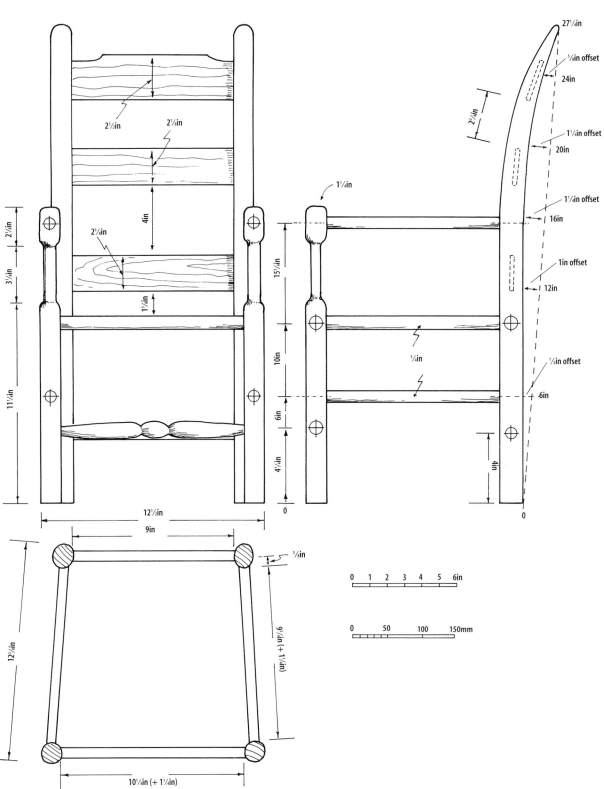

2⅛in

2⅛in

2⅛in

4in

1¼in

2¼in

3⅜in

11¼in

12½in

9in

12⅞in

9¼in (+ 1¼in)

10¼in (+ 1¼in)

1¼in

15½in

10in

6in

4¼in

0

¾in

4in

0

⅝in

27¼in

⅝in offset

24in

1¼in offset

20in

1¼in offset

16in

1in offset

12in

⅛in offset

6in

2¾in

5⁄16in

0   1   2   3   4   5   6in

0   50   100   150mm

OAK CHEST

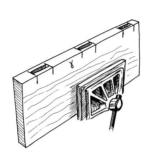

This oak chest represents a deliberate attempt to reproduce an antique. It is a copy of a oak chest that had been kept in a dark corner of my local church for several centuries. It was probably made in the late sixteenth century and used for storing church valuables, which would explain the large number of locks and metal straps.

I will describe how the chest was built with hand tools, including using an adze. It took me 40 hours; if you want to do it more quickly, use machines. Unfortunately, the original

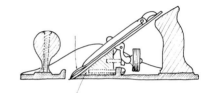

chest has been stolen, so I am unable to show a picture of them side by side.

Apart from the front, which is panelled, the rest of the chest is made from flat boards nailed or pegged together. Of all the components, only the back is cut from a single board; the others have been joined and are held with loose tenons.

The metalwork is perhaps the most striking feature of the chest. The reproductions were beautifully and inexpensively made by a Nailsworth blacksmith called David Tigwell, whose address is in the back of the book.

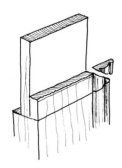

The finished thickness of the planks varies slightly, but it averages about 1⅛in (28mm). The outside surfaces are finished with a plane, but the inside surfaces are either sawn or cut with an adze. Adzes are still made and stocked by tool suppliers.

METHOD

1   Select the best boards for the top and ends. Choose clean, knot-free timber for the framing because you will be cutting out mortises and scratching mouldings, and grain irregularities are a handicap. Reserve the boards with the most confused grain for the panels and keep the knotty and split wood for the bottom and back.

Cut all the pieces to size with a handsaw. Join the boards to make up the widths required for the top, sides, back and bottom. If necessary, shoot the joints, and use loose tenons to hold the planks together (Fig. 1).

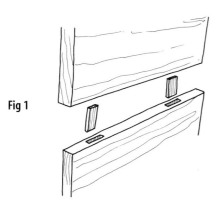

Fig 1

2   Mark in pencil and scratch in the moulding for the front framework. The munting has to be moulded on both outside edges (Fig. 2).

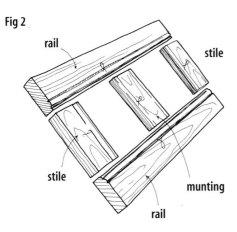

Fig 2

rail

stile

stile

munting

rail

Using the same face side, plough a groove in the edge of the planks (Fig. 3).

Fig 3

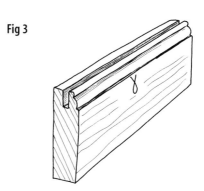

Cut the two stiles to length and the munting, remembering to add the length for the tenons at each end.

Cut the top and bottom rail to length, and mark out and cut the joints (see Special Skills).

3   Cut and fit the panels. Plane their front faces, and finish the back with the side axe. Mullett the edges of the panel, and then assemble the front framework. Drive in wooden pegs to hold it together (Fig. 4, see also Fig 10, page 88).

Fig 4

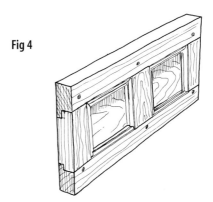

When the front framework is finished, mark out the side planks, taking the overall height and depth of the front frame from the finished piece. The recess at the front end of each plank can be sawn exactly to size (Fig. 5).

Fig 5

width

height
of front

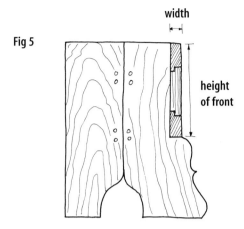

4   Mark out the grids and make a template of the
     unusual curved front edge of the side planks. Saw
     them out with a jigsaw or with a bowsaw. If you use
     a jigsaw, smooth off the saw cut with sandpaper and
     then scrape the teeth of a handsaw around the saw
     cut to reproduce the irregular marks of a bowsaw.

5   Cut the back board and the bottom board to length
     and width.

     The bottom and the back are fixed to the ends
     with nails. Mark the location of the bottom plank
     on the inside of the side planks. Lightly tack a
     couple of battens to hold the bottom in position,
     and pre-drill the nail holes in the side. Make certain
     that the front edge of the bottom plank is perfectly
     aligned with the front edge of the sides and nail it
     in place (Fig. 6).

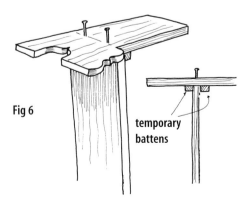

Fig 6

temporary
battens

Reinforce the joint with a diagonal batten and,
after adequately supporting the end you have just
fastened, stand it on end and nail on the opposite
end in the same way (Fig. 7).

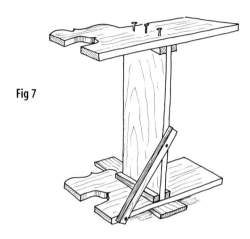

Fig 7

Now nail on the back after pre-drilling all the
nail holes.

The front framework is fastened to the front
with foxed pegs. Instructions for pegging are on
page 19. Cheat and use a little PVA glue along the
joint as well as the pegs to hold it.

6   Carve the simple moulding around the top of the
     chest and then fit the top to the hinges. Because the
     hinges are hand made and are likely to vary slightly
     in size, make the top a little deeper than is shown in
     the drawings. The back edge can always be trimmed
     back to fit the hinges.

7   Before fitting the hinges and waxing the chest, you
     need to colour it and add some marks to suggest a
     venerable age. Round off all the hard, sharp edges,
     roughen up and wear away the lower parts of the
     front and back feet and, perhaps, drill a few
     woodworm holes. Early oak furniture is not usually
     delicate and fragile, and oak church furniture more
     than any other seems to survive 300 years or more
     without suffering much accidental or woodworm

damage. If you are going to have a few woodworm holes, drill them in the white sapwood at the edges of the planks.

8   Finally fit the hinges. Hold them in the required position temporarily with short, ½in (12mm), twin-thread wood screws. These will be later replaced with large-headed reproduction nails. When you come to fit the nails, replace one screw at a time so that the hinge remains exactly where you want it.

FINISHING

You can probably tell by its colour that the chest has been fumed in ammonia gas. Fumed oak, and a lot of old oak that has not been heavily waxed, is a slightly greenish-grey.

To fume a piece of furniture you have to seal it in an airtight bag with a dish or two of ammonia. Because of the high natural content of tannic acid (which reacts with the ammonia), oak turns dark readily. Unless the dishes obstruct the circulation of air in the bag, the colour change will be even and deep. Wherever the ammonia can seep, it will change the colour of the wood and, given time and plenty of replenishment, the ammonia will change the wood colour throughout its thickness.

Take great care when handling ammonia. Try to fume a piece outside. Wear protective goggles and avoid inhaling the fumes. Do not splash the ammonia on your skin.

Fuming alone is not a satisfactory way of reproducing the colour of an old piece of furniture. The surfaces of an antique are mottled, with slight variations of tone and depth of colour. This is true of old oak, walnut, mahogany and other woods, and it is due partly to the effect of light on the timber and to the stains that have been used, many of which are fugitive. Fuming gives a finish that is too regular and often too dark.

The best way to create this mottled effect is to mask off the wood with an easily controlled fluid or cream. I have found that tomato ketchup is an excellent mask. Thick deposits are almost 100 per cent effective in eliminating the effects of the ammonia, while it can be run, dribbled and ragged thinly, giving fine and subtle variations of tone.

The problem with ketchup is that in these circumstances it would have been too good. When the chest was washed clean, some areas would be found to be uncoloured, and then they would have had to be stained. This would not have been a problem if, for example, we had been attempting to achieve a mottled, warm brown colour for the chest. A single coat of brown stain would have coloured the areas that had been heavily masked, and unified its appearance. But this chest had to be greenish-grey.

To provide a less effective mask I used a thinner sauce – a commercial variety of brown sauce – and used a rag to dab and pull over the surfaces. I left some areas heavily covered (particularly edges and corners) and others barely touched.

I wrapped the chest in clear polythene, sealing its edges with masking tape and brown parcel tape, then slit the sheets in three places and gently lowered in small dishes of ammonia. I immediately sealed the slits with masking tape.

The chest was exposed to the fumes for no more than an hour before I opened the bag and emptied the dishes. After a while, when the smell of the ammonia and sauce mix was tolerable, I quickly scrubbed the chest with warm water and soap. The result was not as dark as I wanted – longer exposure would have given that – but the mottling was exactly right.

However, a piece that is fumed is darker than it seems, and a splash of water or finishing spirit will reveal the extent of the colour change. As soon as I rubbed in the wax, it revealed a greater depth of colour than would have been thought.

After fuming and before waxing, replace the hinges. Hold them with screws and then substitute nails. Clench the nails over on the inside of the box (see Tip to the right).

Iron reacts with the tannic acid in oak and corrodes, causing a black stain. Use a little Indian ink to reproduce these black smudges, both on the inside and outside.

Wax the chest with warm brown or black wax to bring up the colour of the wood. When the wax has hardened, follow with really dry, hard black wax – the brittle residue left in an old tin is ideal – and this can be rubbed hard into the grain and into the carvings, and it can be burnished to a hard shine without pulling out of the grain.

The ironwork will now look glaringly new. Mix up a little dry colour pigment – brown umber with a touch of Venetian red – in a teaspoon of water and add a squeeze of PVA glue. The consistency of the mixture should resemble gloss paint. Paint this onto the ironwork and dab it off again with a soft, close-woven cloth. Leave it to dry. Subsequent wax coatings will slowly remove the paint, but by then it will not be noticeable.

TIPS

• Whenever you use pegs to draw joints together or when you are going to wedge them, the pegs should be riven (split) for maximum strength, not sawn.

• When you choose a moulding that will be mitred, choose one that has a clearly defined width, or it will have to be defined with a cutting gauge when the tenon is fitted.

• Cut the back shoulder of the tenon accurately and leave it. Adjustments to improve the fit of the mitres and face shoulder can be made until the back shoulder is hard against the stile. Then you must leave the joint.

• To clench a nail, hold a dolly (lump of metal) against the nail point as it emerges through the oak. The dolly will bend the nail back against or into the side of the plank.

SPECIAL SKILLS

LOOSE TENONS

Fitted about 18in (457mm) apart, a row of loose tenons will secure an edge joint. Place the planks that are to be joined in position across a pair of trestles. Cut a strip of straight-grained wood, about ³⁄₈in (10mm) thick and 2in (50mm) wide, from which you can saw the tenons. Mark face sides of each plank and the positions of each tenon with a freehand mark that crosses the join between both planks (Fig. 8).

Fig 8

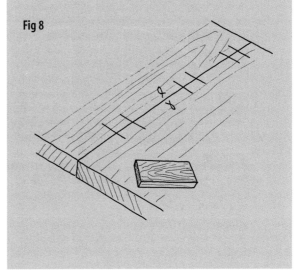

Take one plank at a time, square across the marks and, using the router fitted with a ³⁄₈ in (10mm) cutter, plunge out a mortise between the marks (Fig. 9). Cut out all the mortises on the first edge, and then take the next plank and cut the matching mortises. Fit the tenons in the mortises and check that the planks pull together well.

Secure one row of tenons with pegs, then draw the second plank up tight using draw pegs.

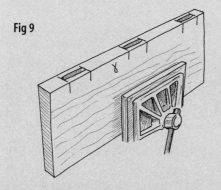

Fig 9

DRAW PEGS

Draw pegs are a useful way of pulling a mortise and tenon joint up tight, although using them takes longer than gluing and clamping a joint.

Cut the mortise and tenon joint in the normal way and make sure the pieces fit together. Separate the joint, and slip an offcut of wood into the mortise to protect the inside of the mortise from damage. Drill a peghole through the mortise, and remove the offcut from the mortise (Fig. 10). Insert the tenon and, with it in place, mark the centre for the peg hole in the tenon. It is offset slightly – ¹⁄₁₆ in (1mm) closer to the shoulder of the joint (Fig. 11).

Remove the tenon and drill the peghole. When the tenon is replaced, the joint will look as illustrated in Fig. 12, and when a tapered peg is driven into the hole, it will pull the tenon tighter into the mortise (Fig. 13).

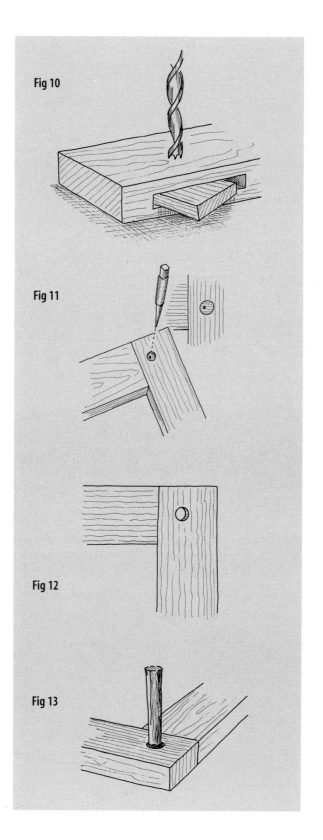

Fig 10

Fig 11

Fig 12

Fig 13

MARKING AND CUTTING A MITRED MORTISE AND TENON JOINT

If you look carefully at the photograph of the chest, you will see how the joints in the front frame fit to give a continuous moulded edge round each panel. This is quite a tricky joint to cut well, but you will find the mitre guide illustrated in Fig. 17 to be a great help in achieving a good fit. This joint is known as a true mitre. It is one of several means of running two mouldings together, and it can be seen on chests and panels made as long ago as the mid-fifteenth century. Then, as today, there appears to have been a variety of ways of coping with the technical problems of joining mouldings at right angles.

Prepare the wood for joining. Finish the mouldings and plough the groove.

At first, the joint is laid out in the same way as an ordinary mortise and tenon joint, except that only the inside shoulder of the tenon is incised with a knife. The outer (face-side) shoulder is left pencilled.

Use the marking gauge to scribe the sides of the tenon (Fig. 14), and use a 45 degree mitre square to mark off the mitre on the edge of the tenon.

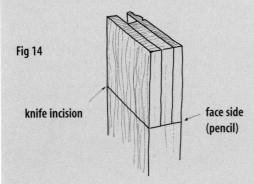

Fig 14

knife incision — face side (pencil)

Start the mitre at the shoulder line and extend it across the face side of the tenon (Fig. 15). Incise this line with a knife.

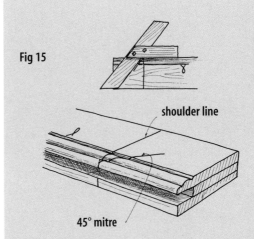

Fig 15

shoulder line

45° mitre

Where the mitre lines cross beyond the moulding onto the flat surface of the face side, square across with the set square. This 45 degree line and its lower shoulder are the shoulder lines that you cut to on the face side.

Saw down the sides of the tenon, and remove the inside shoulder with a tenon saw. Trim back to the scribe line with a rebate plane if necessary. Remove the opposite cheek, trimming well clear of the shoulder line.

Saw the 45 degree mitre with the tenon saw, keeping well clear of the line (Fig. 16). Trim back to the line with a sharp bevel-edge chisel, using the home-made mitre template illustrated in Fig. 17 to guide the chisel blade.

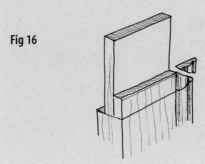

Fig 16

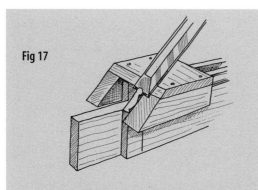

Fig 17

Trim the shoulder line square (Fig. 18) and cut out the haunch at the back edge of the tenon. With the munting, where there is a groove each side, such a haunch will be unnecessary.

Fig 18

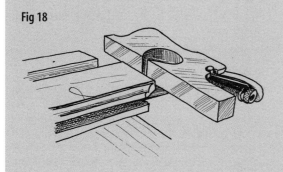

Now cut out the mortise. This will start in the groove on one side and between the gauged lines on the back. When the mortise has been cut and driven clean, fit the tenon. The joint will look as illustrated in Fig. 19. You will see that if the initial marking out of the mortise and tenon joint is clear, the subsequent adjustment of the join to take the tenon is straightforward.

Scribe the 45 degree mitre on the stile and cut close to it with a 90 degree saw cut (Fig. 20). Shave the mitre to the scribe line, again using the mitre template, and then clear away the waste until the tenon sits tightly and the mouldings merge (Fig. 21).

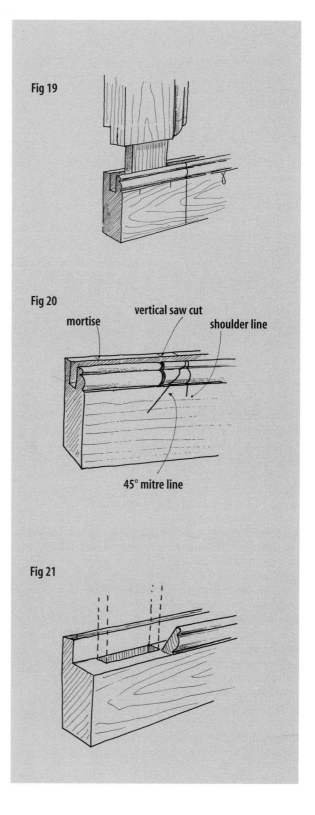

Fig 19

Fig 20

mortise · vertical saw cut · shoulder line

45° mitre line

Fig 21

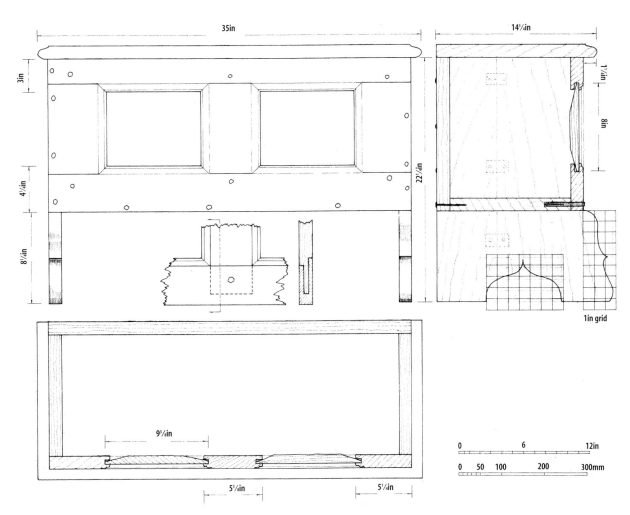

1in grid

0   6   12in

0   50   100   200   300mm

CUTTING LIST

Oak Chest (nominal sizes: in/mm)

Item	Quantity	Length	Width	Thickness
Top	2	35/890	8/200	1½/38
Back	2	33/838	8/200	1½/38
Bottom	2	31/790	6/150	1½/38
Sides	4	23/585	9/230	1½/38
Panels	2	10/255	8½/215	1/25
Rail	1	3/75	4/100	1½/38
Rail	1	33/838	5/127	1½/38
Stiles	3	13/330	6/150	1½/38

SET OF LADDER-
BACK CHAIRS

Ladder-backs are a traditional English style. By the end of the
nineteenth century they were predominantly machine made,
spindly and mean in proportion. These chairs are copies of one made
by Ernest Gimson in 1904 which features a high back and a generous-
sized seat.

These chairs might look as if they have been turned, but, as with the Child's Chair (see page
72), they have been made without a lathe in a batch of four to save
time. Each chair took me an average of 10 hours to make.

When I was making the chairs in batches I found it was helpful to
have strong elastic bands to bundle up similar components.
Combined with special wire hooks, the bands are also useful for

holding the chairs together
while the glue dries.

Select straight-grained wood for all the components.

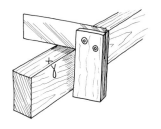

I obtained most of the wood I needed from one rough-sawn
ash plank, 10ft (3m) long, 1⅝in (41mm) thick and about 20in
(510mm) wide.

METHOD

1   Mark out and cut the longest pieces first, aligning them with the grain. Then cut the front legs, rails and stretchers. The back slats can be sawn from offcuts. Cut each piece exactly to length. No advantage is gained by leaving waste at the ends of any of these pieces, but make sure you have measured accurately before you start sawing.

   The backs of the chairs taper slightly, but at this stage, cut the slats all the same length – they can be trimmed before fitting.

   Collect the seat stretchers and trim them quickly to size with the axe. They have a peculiar shape – wide in the middle and fine at the ends, and they bow outwards slightly. This is a strong shape, and if you take care they can be left as finished with the axe (Fig. 1).

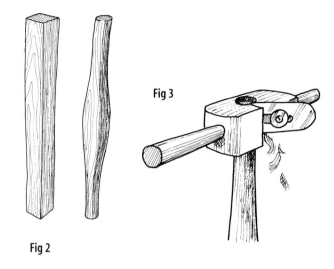

Fig 2

Fig 3

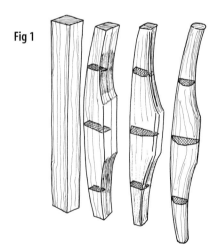

Fig 1

   Collect the front rails and put them to one side. Trim the remaining rails into rough cylinders with the side axe. Shape them carefully with a drawknife, and finish rounding off with a shoulder plane.

   Take the front rail, and trim it to size with the side axe. Finish with the drawer knife and spokeshave (Fig. 2).

   Because shaping the ends individually with a chisel or gouge is both tedious and a rather hit-and-miss process, make a simple two-handed cutter to trim the ends so that they fit exactly into the auger holes (Fig. 3). Trim the ends with the cutter and sand each piece.

2   Mark the height of the seat on all the back legs. This is their greatest diameter, and they taper to the ends.

   Slice off the corners with the side axe, and continue smoothing and rounding with the drawknife. Finish with a plane. Finish the front legs in the same way. These taper from the top. Sand all the legs.

3   There is a simple decoration cut into the top of each leg. Find a short length of brass or galvanized picture wire and thread a handle through a loop at each end. Grip the leg in the vice, loop the wire around the far side and about ⅜in (10mm) below the top, and vigorously pull the ends to and fro for a few moments (Fig. 4). Turn the leg around and complete the groove.

   Repeat with the other legs, then round off the tops of the legs with your penknife. Sand them to finish.

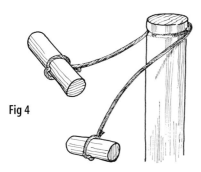

Fig 4

4   Cut out and smooth all the back slats. These are finished quite thin – a little less than ¼in (6mm) is about right – then round off the tops and bottoms, but do not cut them to length.

   To save time, I cut all the mortises with a router, and I made a router box just long enough to hold the back legs (see Special Skill, page 99).

5   Bend the back slats to shape (see page 76). Mark the positions for the rail and stretcher holes on a template stick, then transfer the marks to the legs.

6   Using the jig that is described on page 96 and the ⅝in (16mm) auger bit, drill the holes for the front rail and stretcher of the first pair of legs. Fit them together and sight down them. They should be square and parallel. Adjust them if necessary and glue them together, holding the joints with strong rubber bands (Fig. 5).

Fig 5

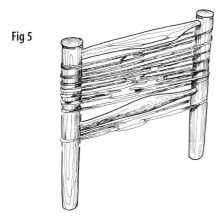

Repeat with the other front legs and leave until the glue hardens.

7   The rails and stretchers have been cut to length, but of the back slats, only the top slat, which is the longest, should fit. Take a piece of board and mark on it, full size, the two splayed back legs in their correct positions relative to each other, and the positions of the slats, stretcher and rail. The inner line of each back leg also represents the shoulder lines of the slats, stretcher and rail (Fig. 6).

Fig 6

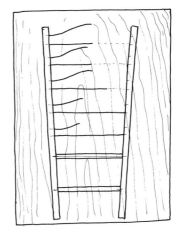

   Mark and drill the holes for the rail and stretcher between the back legs. Because the back legs converge slightly, the holes you drill will be at slightly less than 90 degrees to the leg. Transfer the angle from the board to the sighting board, which is fixed to the bench (Fig. 7). Remember, too, that you should offset the holes slightly to allow for the curve of the back slats (Fig. 8).

8   Put the slats in the mortises of one leg, adjusting them to fit where necessary. Press the stretcher and the rail in place and lay the leg in position on the board.

   Take a straightedge and strike off the shoulder lines for all the slats, referring to the lines drawn on

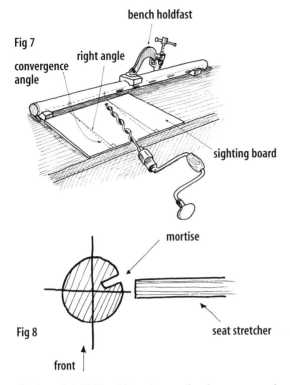

Fig 7

convergence angle

right angle

bench holdfast

sighting board

mortise

Fig 8

seat stretcher

front

the board. Add ½in (12mm) extra for the tenons and cut off the surplus. Trim the ends to fit, then glue and assemble the back, using elastic bands or tourniquets to hold it. Sight across the legs and correct any twist before leaving the glue to harden.

9 Reset the simple jig to hold the front and back pairs of legs while you drill them (Fig. 9). Notice that both sets of legs lean backwards slightly, and you should mark off the angles on the sighting board.

Drill all the remaining holes in the legs, and assemble the chair.

FINISHING

After sanding, the chairs were stained with a mixture of Colron stains. I used English light oak as the base and added a touch of Canadian cedar and American walnut. After applying the stain with a brush I wiped off the surplus with a clean rag.

When the stain was dry, I brushed on two coats

of shellac button polish and finished with a final coat, applied with a rubber cloth dipped in a saucer of shellac. When dry, the chairs were rubbed down with 000 wire wool and waxed with black wax.

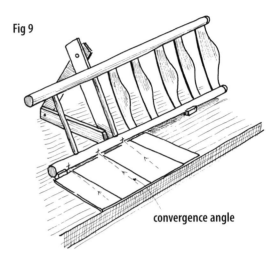

Fig 9

convergence angle

SEATING

Traditionally the chairs would have rush seats, and a full description of the rush seating technique is included in my book *Handbook of Furniture Restoration*. For these chairs I used seagrass instead. It comes in hanks, already spun into a thin rope.

Weaving a seat is easy: just wind the string round the seat stretchers from front to back, and then weave across the seat, grouping the front to back strings in sixes or eights to give a bold chequered pattern.

The only problem is that the seat tapers towards the back, with the front stretcher longer than the one at the back. To make the woven pattern reach the corners, wind the initial front to back turns carefully.

Starting at one front corner, take two turns round the stretcher before running the string round the back and straight back to the front, where you take an extra turn before taking it to the back again (Fig. 10). You repeat this, slowly working towards the centre of the stretchers, until the string, stretched from the front to back is at last square with the stretchers (Fig. 11).

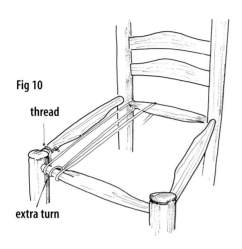

Fig 10

thread

extra turn

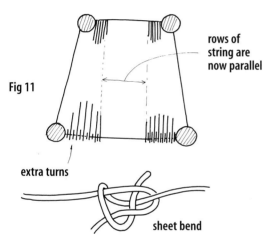

Fig 11

rows of
string are
now parallel

extra turns

sheet bend

From then on you can wind the string evenly round the stretchers, until you approach the opposite corner. Then give the string an extra turn at the front for each one at the back. Pull these front to back strings quite tight. Thread a flexible ruler across the seat, slipping it across six strings then under the next six and so on. Feed the seagrass across, using a long thick wire, with a loop worked into its end, to pull it through (coathanger wire is ideal). Work towards the front, joining the seagrass with a reef knot or a sheet bend when necessary (Fig. 11). As the woven pattern develops you can change the sizes of the squares.

Finish by tying the end of the seagrass to strings under the seat. Tuck the loose ends into the seat.

SPECIAL SKILLS

RE-SAWING A PLANK

This is the process of converting a rough-cut plank into smaller battens. Before you re-saw a plank, inspect it on both sides. If one side is broad and clean, and the other narrower and knotty, mark out your work on the knotty side.

The ash plank I used for making these chairs was fairly straight, and the heartwood, which was split and opened in places, ran more or less up its centre. Because the plank was cut from the widest part of the trunk, it was much the same on its other side. My priority was to obtain wood for the eight back legs. These are the longest and easier to shape if the grain runs true. With four each side of the heartwood, I could mark off the lower, broader part of the plank for the legs. The eight front legs could be obtained from the portion of plank immediately above the back legs.

From then, it was a matter of designating timber for the rails, stretchers and slats, and marking them out with a wax pencil (Fig. 12).

Fig 12

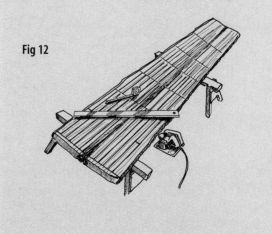

To saw all these pieces by hand would be slow, and it would be difficult and dangerous to cut a plank this size on a small lightweight circular saw. I rested the plank on a pair of trestles, and used a hand-held circular saw.

The plank was cut into lengths, and then the first cuts were made each side of the useless heartwood. These were sawn straight by steering the saw onto the pencilled line (see page 10). From then on the parallel fence was fitted for the remaining cuts.

Once the plank was reduced to small lengths, and the heartwood was sawn out, I used the table-mounted circular saw for cutting the rails and stretchers. The slats were cut as blocks, and sawn by hand into thin, $5/16$ in (7mm), slices.

MAKING AN END CUTTER

As you can see (Fig. 13), this is a simple tool to make. Take a block of hardwood, about $1^3/_4$in (45mm) thick, and bore a $5/_8$in (16mm) hole through the centre.

Mark the bed for the blade, almost at a tangent

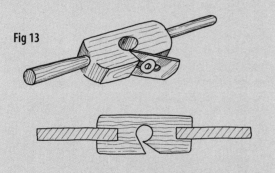

Fig 13

from the hole to the edge of the block, and cut it with a handsaw. Make the second cut, finishing to make a narrow slot at the hole in the centre (Fig. 14). Level the blade-bearing face with a chisel.

I used a shoulder plane blade for the cutter, holding it in position with a round-headed wood screw

bearing against a steel washer (Fig. 15). If you have not got a discarded blade that is suitable, you can buy replacement blades from most tool stores. Fit the two dowel handles into holes drilled into the block.

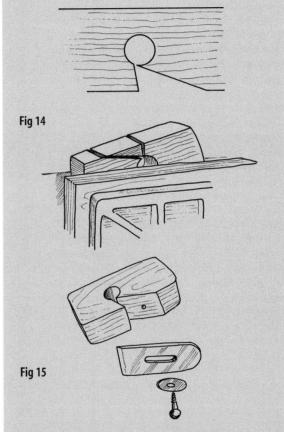

Fig 14

Fig 15

When you use it, you might find that the blade does not feed easily into wood that is too thick. Remove the blade and grind the curved corner to it, and replace it with the curved part offsetting the bottom edge of the block (Fig. 16). This should remove the larger obstructions and enable the cutter to feed more easily.

Remember that this is only a tool for shaving the ends to size. It will not give a satisfactory finish if you run it right down the rail.

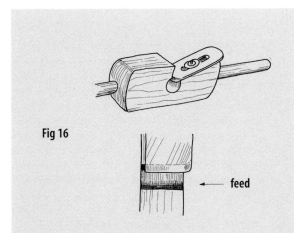

Fig 16

← feed

MORTISING THE LEGS WITH A ROUTER

The bottom of the simple router box illustrated in Fig. 17 is set down from the top edge by a fraction more than the diameter of the leg (Fig. 18).

Fig 17

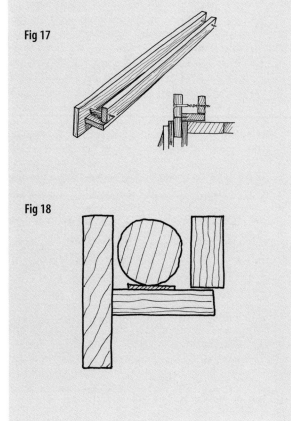

Fig 18

One side of the box is arranged so that the vice will grip the side, with the bottom of the box resting on the bench. The middle section of the opposite side is nailed to the bottom, but the ends are left unfastened and are pulled in tight by countersunk twin-thread wood screws (Fig. 19).

Fig 19

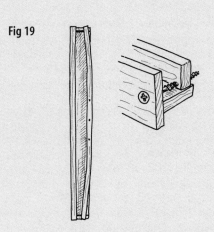

Grip the box in the vice and place a back leg in it. Nail a narrow block at each end to locate the leg. Prop the ends of the leg so that the top edge is flush with, or a little below, the level of the sides and clamp it. If the clamp is applied to the part of the leg below the stretchers, it will not be in the way of the router (Fig. 20).

Fig 20

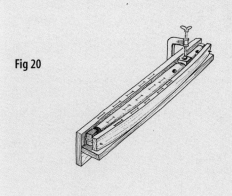

Draw the ends of the box tight against the chair leg, using the twin-thread screws.

Fit the router with a $\frac{1}{4}$in (6mm) router bit and its adjustable parallel fence. Position it as illustrated (Fig. 21) and adjust the depth stop to give a plunge depth of slightly more than is required. Mark accurately on the side of the box the position for the top of the leg, and the length and position of each slat mortise so that each leg can be marked up from the box once it is positioned properly.

Using the router, cut each mortise, plunging out about $\frac{1}{8}$in (2mm) or slightly more each time.

Fig 21

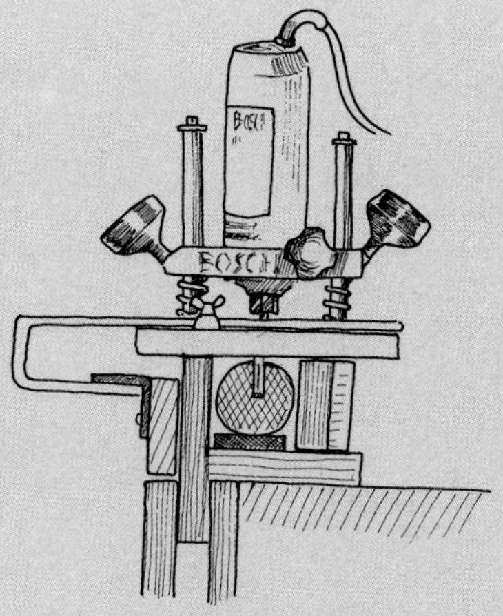

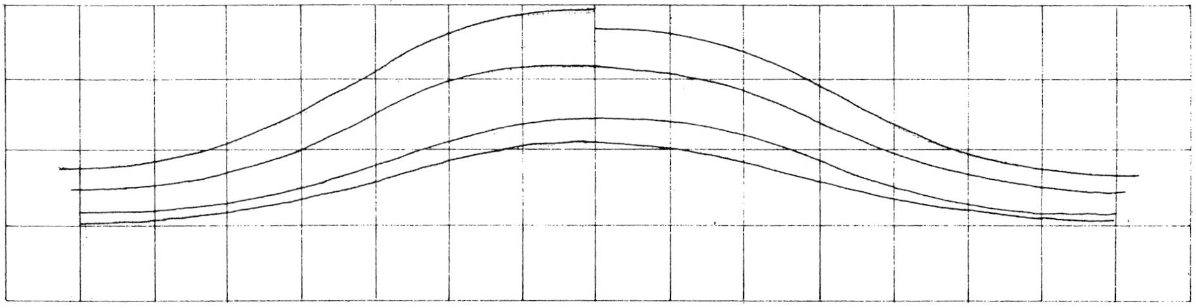

1in grid

CUTTING LIST

Ladder-back Chair (nominal sizes: in/mm)

Item	Quantity	Length	Width	Thickness
Back legs	2	$40\frac{1}{4}$/1022	$1\frac{1}{2}$/38	$1\frac{1}{2}$/38 Straight ash/oak
Front legs	2	$18\frac{1}{2}$/470	$1\frac{5}{8}$/41	$1\frac{5}{8}$/41
Rails	5	14/356	$\frac{3}{4}$/19	$\frac{3}{4}$/19
Seat stretchers	4	$18\frac{1}{2}$/470	2/50	1/25
Front rail	1	$18\frac{1}{2}$/470	$1\frac{1}{2}$/38	$1\frac{1}{2}$/38
Slats	5	15/380	$3\frac{3}{4}$/95	$\frac{1}{4}$/6

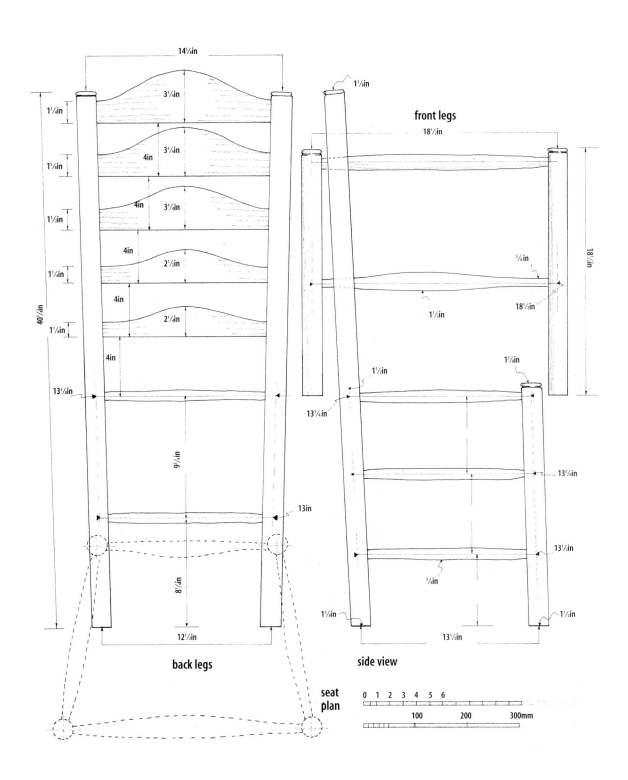

back legs

side view

front legs

seat
plan

0 1 2 3 4 5 6
100   200   300mm

S L E I G H   B E D

This is a classic continental-style sleigh bed. The one illustrated is a single width, and it can be used as a settee or day-bed because the rounded, comfortable ends are the right height for armrests.

It is made of yew. The rich brown colour and the strongly marked swirling grain patterns are characteristic of yew, and the colour will deepen as the wood ages. It is finished with linseed oil rubbed into the grain. Yew has a fine, silky texture, but it is difficult to work, and even what appear to be good planks can be riddled with splits or shakes. It is partly because of

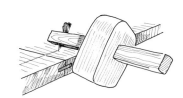

this that I had to incorporate discrete reinforcement pads into the bed.

The planking from which it was made is slightly less than 1in (25mm) thick, and although the legs are short and stocky, the framework is likely to be subjected to a great deal of wear and tear. The legs are reinforced on the inside with ¼in (6mm) plywood strips, and the mortise and tenon joints holding the sides to the ends are also reinforced on the inside.

METHOD

1   Draw a cardboard template of one endboard. Square it up using the grid marked on the drawings and mark on the template the top and bottom transverse boards and the panel between them. Also mark the exact position and shape of the groove that locates the ends and the screw holes that are needed to secure them (Fig. 1).

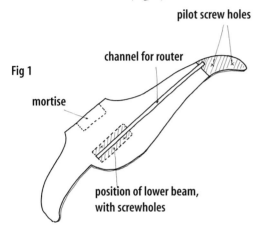

Fig 1

pilot screw holes

channel for router

mortise

position of lower beam, with screwholes

2   The serpentine boards for the ends are very wide, and you will have to make up the width by gluing additional wood to the edges. Note that the full shape of the endboard is not cut out of the solid, partly because it would be too weak and partly because the ends would not look so fine. Instead, the sides are tenoned into a strong part of the leg, and earpieces are glued above and beneath them (Fig. 2).

Once you have made the template, assemble and glue together the boards making up the ends.

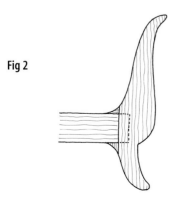

Fig 2

2   While the glue in the ends is hardening, find enough wood to make up the tops of the headboards. The template for shaping them can be traced from the top of the end template you have just made.

Fig. 3 shows how these boards are made up. You do not have to do it this way, but bear in mind, first, that it is better if the curved upper face of the board is clear of joins and, second, that you will want to arrange the pieces to minimize the labour in shaping it.

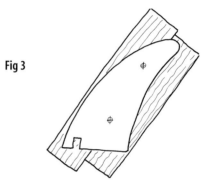

Fig 3

Glue the top planks together with either an epoxy or a urea-formaldehyde glue such as Cascamite. Epoxy is preferable because it is stronger and does not contain water, which might cause the balks to warp as they are drying.

3   Cut the endboards to shape with a jigsaw fitted with a T 144D blade. Smooth the ends with a spokeshave, rasp or 60 grit sandpaper backed by a wood block and finish with a cabinet scraper.

Mark on the inside face of each endboard the groove and the positions for the screws holding the headboards (Fig. 4). These screw holes are close to, but do not pass through, the grooves. Drill the screw holes with a ⅛in (2mm) drill.

4   Next cut out the groove. You will need a plywood or medium density fibreboard template for this, and you use it in conjunction with the router guide

Fig 4

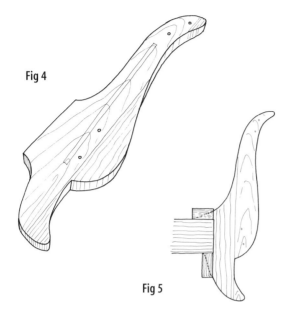

Fig 5

plate, which is fitted to the faceplate of the router (see Special Skill, page 109).

Nail the template to the first endboard and cut the groove. Vacuum up any dust and repeat with the other boards.

Cut the mortise and tenon joints that join the sides to the ends. Glue the joints together and fit the small earpieces, which were made from offcuts, into position above and below each joint (Fig. 5). Hold them in place with masking tape and rubber bands until the glue is dry, then plane them all flush and, after marking with the template, saw them to shape.

5   Cut to length the two transverse beams at each end. Mark them in pairs. The lower beam at each end of the bed has a tongue worked in its end (which locates in the groove), and this has to be added to its overall length, but the shoulder lines remain the same.

Saw the bottom of each pair to length and saw out the tongue, using the circular saw for the shoulder cut and a chisel for trimming the sides (Fig. 6).

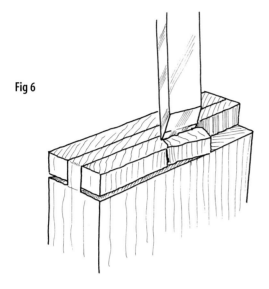

Fig 6

6   Collect together enough thin planks to make the panelling at each end. Join them with loose tongues, cutting the slots for the tongues either on the circular saw or with a plough plane. Assemble the panels together, holding them tightly with many strips of masking tape strapped to each side. Take each panel at a time, and fence it on three sides with thin wooden battens pinned to the bench, leaving the top clear for smoothing and one edge slightly overhanging the bench. The masking tape and fence will hold the panels steady while you mark and trim the tops level and sand and scrape their faces smooth (Fig. 7)

Mark and cut the rebate around the edge of the panel (see Tip, page 109).

Fig 7

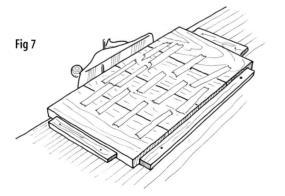

7   Roughly shape the top end bars of the bed. First, plane the bottom edge to its true angle and mark on each end the outline of the section (Fig. 8).

The concave side is shaped next. Hold the bar in a furniture clamp and grip the clamp in the vice (Fig. 9). Removing all the waste from this side will seem quite an awesome prospect, but it is easy if you fit a sharp ⅜in (10mm) cutter in the router and rout along the plank, lowering the router in steps as the amount of waste increases. When you reach the centre of the plank, leave a strip about ³⁄₁₆in (5mm) wide to support the router and remove the waste on the other side.

Fig 8

Fig 9

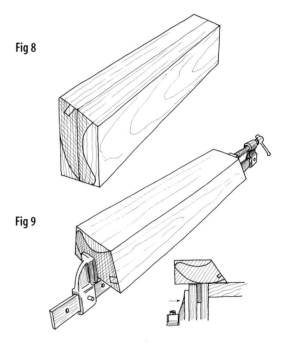

Take a gouge and fair the curve, removing all the hard edges. Then use a curved scraper to remove the rest of the wood. Finish with a drum sander powered by the electric drill (Fig. 10).

Turn the bar over, fasten it in the clamp and plane it to within ¹⁄₁₆in (1mm) of the finished line. The final shaping of the outside is completed after the ends are assembled.

The bed is almost ready for assembly.

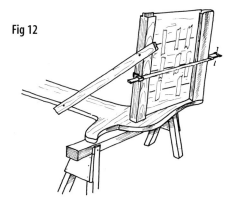

Fig 12

8   Use the circular saw to cut the groove in the top
edge of the lower beams and the bottom edge of
the top beams. If you use the same setting for each
groove, you need to reset the saw fence only once
(Fig. 11).

Fig 10

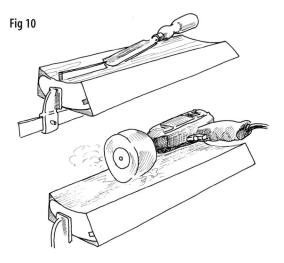

Fig 11   2nd cut   1st cut   table   saw blade

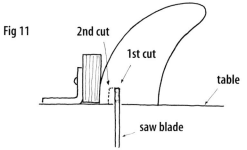

Rest a side across a pair of trestles, inside facing
upwards, and assemble one pair of end beams, with
the panel held between them. Lift it into position
and hold it in place with a diagonal batten (Fig. 12).
Do the same at the other end. Lift the other side
plank onto the upright ends and tap it into place.

If everything fits – except for the top board at
each end, which will be a little proud – you can fix
it all together.

If you are only going to use screws at this stage
to hold the ends together, they should be long and
substantial – 4in (100mm) slotted and countersunk
twin-thread screws will do. The positions for the

screw holes should be visible from the outside of the
end frames. The small diameter holes bored earlier
indicate the centres for the screws (see step 3).

Counterbore the screw holes so that the heads
can be recessed by ⅜in (10mm) and drill the long
pilot holes for each screw. If you are fastening
hardwood, do not make the pilot holes too small or
short, because the threads of these screws are deep
compared with the diameter of the shank, and if you
apply too much force you will shear off the head.

Once the joints are pulled up tight (and after
the glue has dried), trim the top of the end planks
flush with the shaped ends using a plane or an
electric belt sander.

9   Glue and nail a supporting batten around the inside
of the bed (Fig. 13) and fit the supporting gussets
on the insides of the corners. Fit additional plates
behind the mortise and tenon joint if necessary.

Fig 13

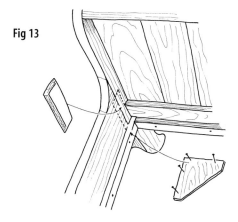

Fit the plywood bottom board and screw it in position.

If you are going to dismantle the bed in order to move it into a bedroom, wait until it is in position before plugging the screw holes. Cut the plugs using a ½in (12mm) or ⅝in (16mm) plug cutter (Fig. 14). Before fitting the plugs take a matchstick and spot the top of each screw with some grease, butter or tallow. Tap the plugs into the holes with glue. Plane and sand them flush when the glue has dried. If you need to remove the plugs, knock a screwdriver into the centre of each and lever it out.

Fig 14

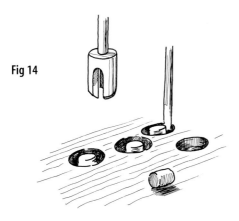

FINISHING

I used an oil finish on the bed featured in the photographs. This is a hard-wearing, resilient finish, which burnishes and improves with use. I have included a little information on this finish here, but I do not recommend it for use with softwoods. There are easier ways of making pine furniture look attractive, and one of these is described here.

Oil Finish

As well as linseed oil, there are commercial preparations for an oil finish using tung and other oils that are as satisfactory. Follow the instructions that are supplied with the oil.

Before you apply the finish, complete all the colouring in of patches and staining. Water colours and spirit stains can be used for colouring small areas, and water-, chemical- or spirit-based stains are suitable for overall staining. Do not use an oil-based stain, which might bleed into the finish.

Take some boiled linseed oil and heat gently in a double boiler to thin. For deeper and quicker penetration add a little turpentine and, for faster drying, add 20 per cent oil-based varnish.

Pour the oil onto a soft, absorbent cloth and rub it over the bed. Rub quite hard until there is none left on the surface. Leave the wood to dry.

Repeat this once a day for a week. The wood will turn darker and a sheen will begin to appear on its surface. Continue the process once a week for a month, and then once a month for the rest of the year. Eventually, the oil and constant burnishing will produce a bright, polished finish in the surface of the wood that is resistant to heat and spirit stains and is flexible enough not to be damaged by bruising.

Stain and Shellac Finish

If you used pine or another softwood, sand the bed, finishing with 220 or 240 grit paper. Mix up a stain using Colron dyes. Start by pouring a large quantity of English light oak, a light yellowish-brown colour, into a glass bottle. Add a small quantity of Canadian cedar, which is red, to warm up the mixture. Add a dash of American walnut, which is warm brown, mix them together and use a rag to apply the mixture all over the bed.

Watch out for the end grain at the ends of the bed, indicated with arrows in Fig 15. This will absorb more than its fair share of the stain, and if you are not careful will turn too dark. Do not stain these areas until your rag is almost exhausted and tip a little English light oak onto the same rag, before quickly wiping the ends.

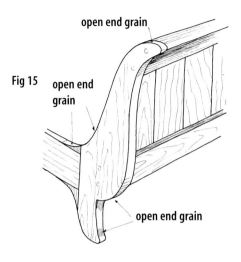

Fig 15 open end grain

open end grain

open end grain

Leave the stain to dry for about 20 minutes, and then, even if the wood is still slightly damp, follow with a brush coat of orange button polish shellac, also applied with the grain. Allowing at least 30 minutes between coats, build up the finish, perhaps applying four or five coats altogether.

Leave the bed to dry for a day, and then use a large wad of 0000 wire wool to smooth all the surfaces. Bring the work to a good polish with a hard, quick-drying wax.

TIP

When rebating incise each cut with a cutting gauge, before cutting the rebate with a router. This gives a cleaner cut (Fig. 16).

Fig 16

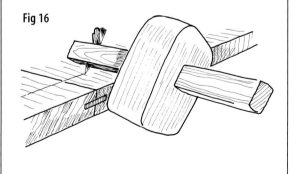

SPECIAL SKILL

USING A ROUTER GUIDE PLATE

The router guide plate is positioned as shown in Fig. 17. Its purpose is to provide a fence adjacent to, and equidistant from, the cutter, and it allows the router to be used with freedom inside a fixed hardboard or plywood template.

Fig 17

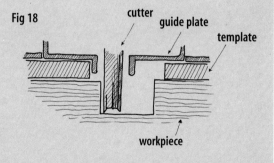

A disadvantage of the guide plate is that the cutter you use has to be small enough to fit through the plate. You will notice that there is about $1/8$in (2mm) offset between the edge of the cutter and the outer (bearing) edge of the guide plate (Fig. 18).

Fig 18   cutter   guide plate   template

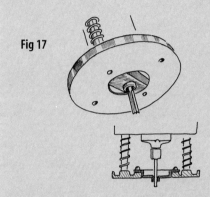

workpiece

When you are marking the size of the template slot, you must add this additional measurement to the dimensions you use so that the groove is the required width.

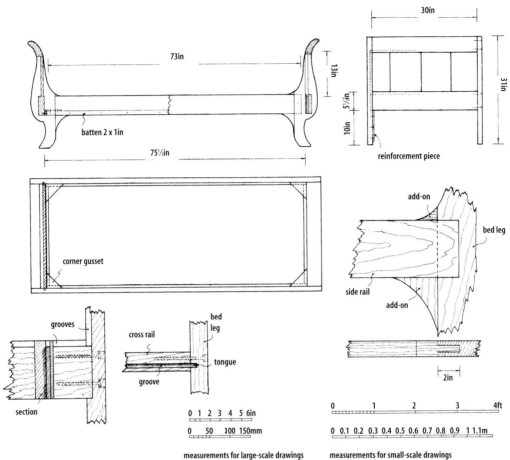

measurements for large-scale drawings

measurements for small-scale drawings

CUTTING LIST

Sleigh Bed (nominal sizes: in/mm)

Item	Quantity	Length	Width	Thickness
Sides	2	73/1855	6/150	$1\frac{1}{4}$/32
Ends – legs	4	31/790	7/178	$1\frac{1}{4}$/32
Add-ons				Offcuts
Top beam, to make	2	30/760	7/178	3/75
Bottom beam	2	30/760	6/150	2/50
Panel, to make		13/330	30/760	¾/19
Battens	2	73/1855	2/50	1/25
	2	30/760	2/50	1/25
Plywood	1	76/1930	30/760	¼/6 Low grade

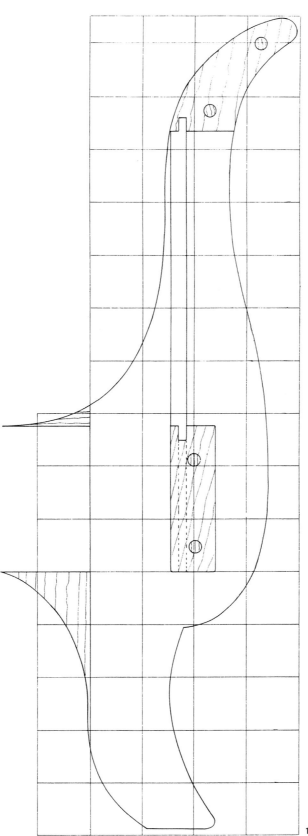

1in grid

KITCHEN DRESSER

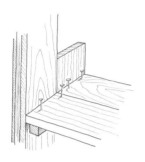

This must be one of the easiest dressers to make. It is a copy of an ancient and derelict Irish dresser, and it is made from standard sized planks of fir. It took about 50 hours to make, and the wood was not expensive. The carcass is held together with galvanized nails and glue.

Designing a frieze is probably harder than cutting one out. I have suggested a section of frieze in the illustrations, and there is a squared grid to help anyone who wants to copy it. You might like to adapt it, by including elements that

reflect your life – dates and initials are often incorporated in these simple sawn patterns, or you might want birds or animals, such as mice, running around the edge. When you are thinking of the design, try to contain it inside the width of the plank (only the wheel required an extra piece glued on), and avoid sharp pieces that will get broken.

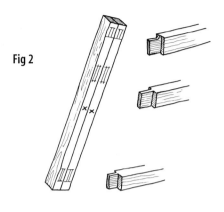

Fig 2

METHOD

1 Select straight clean planks for the sides of the dresser, rebate the back edge on each side, cut them to length and lay them together, ready for gluing.

Mark off the positions for the battens, squaring across the planks to ensure they will be accurately placed. Glue the edges of the boards, clamp them together and nail on the battens.

When the glue has dried, plane up the outer faces of the sides and saw the feet at the bottom with a jigsaw (Fig. 1).

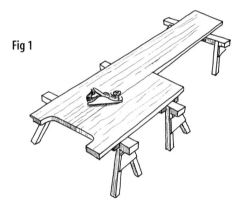

Fig 1

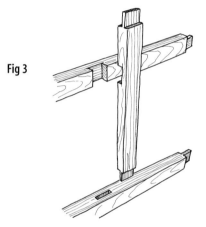

Fig 3

2 Make the front frame, which is held together with mortise and stub tenons, in the following order. First, cut the sides and centre plank to length, then cut the rails to length.

Clamp the sides together, and mark off the positions for the mortises. The mortise in the top is stopped short of the top (Fig. 2). Clamp the rails together and mark off the shoulders for the tenons.

Set the mortise gauge to the thickness of your ⅜in (10mm) mortise chisel (or router bit, if you are going to rout out these mortises, see page 65), and mark and saw the tenons. Cut out the mortises, fit the tenons and number the joints.

Assemble the framework, knock the joints tight, and check the diagonals.

Put the centre plank in place, and mark off the positions for all the joints with a sharp pencil.

There is a mortise and tenon joint at the ends, and the joint in the middle is a cross-halving joint (Fig. 3).

Complete the marking out of the joints with the pieces separated, and cut them out. Instructions for cutting a cross-halving joint are on page 118.

Assemble the framework, fitting the centre division first and then the sides. Check that it all fits together before gluing it. Drive a panel pin through each tenon to hold the joints. Check the diagonals and make sure the frame is square before leaving it to dry.

3 Cut the planks that make up the worktop and bottom shelf roughly to size. Glue them and hold them on the underside with a couple of 1in (25mm) battens.

Check that the doorframe has been made the correct width. The doorframe should be the width of the dresser, and the shelves are the total width, less the thickness of two sides. If the doorframe is wrong, adjust the length of the shelves.

Trim all the shelves, the top, the worktop and the bottom exactly to length with a handsaw.

Check that the shelves lie flush with the front planks and level with the base of the rebate at the back (Fig. 4). Trim the back edges with a circular saw or plane if necessary.

Fig 4

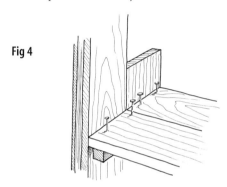

4   Glue and nail one side to the bottom board and support the side with a diagonal brace tacked to the front. Glue and nail on the opposite side, and support it with a diagonal.

Glue and place the worktop in position, and pull the tops of the sides together with a tourniquet to close the joint, which you can then nail (Fig. 5). Glue and fasten the remaining shelves and the top.

Fig 5

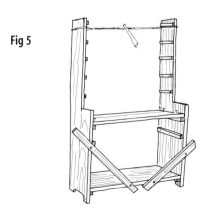

Make sure that the dresser is true and square before nailing on the tongue and grooving at the back, and gluing and nailing the doorframe to the front of the dresser.

5   Make the frieze. First fit the frieze plank, which is notched at the bottom edge to fit over the worktop endboard and is fastened to the sideplanks (Fig. 6).

Cut and fit both side pieces. It is probably a good idea to make the recess slightly deeper than necessary, so that the edge of the frieze plank overhangs the sides, and can be planed flush after fitting (Fig. 7).

Fig 6

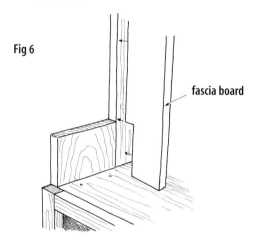

fascia board

Fig 7

overhang →

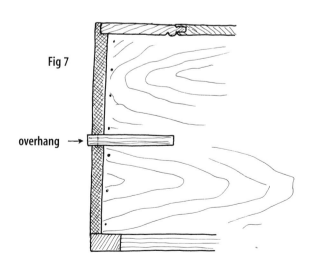

115

Cut a piece for the horizontal part of the frieze, about 3in (75mm) longer than the distance between the uprights to allow for the cross-halving joint. Hold it in position and mark off the shoulders for the cross-halving joint on both the verticals and the horizontal part of the frieze (Figs. 8 and 9).

Cut out the cross-halving joints and tack the three boards in place (see Special Skills, page 118).

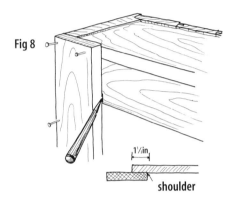

Fig 8

1¹⁄₂in

shoulder

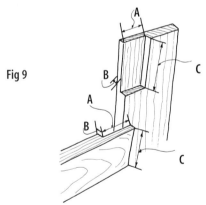

Fig 9

6   Draw the frieze design to full size on stiff paper and cut it out with a scalpel. Transfer the drawing to the wood with a ball-point pen. Fit a fine, narrow blade to your jigsaw (T 119BO) and cut it out. Do not cut the areas close to the cross-halving joint, which should be left until the frieze is glued together.

When the frieze is sawn out, glue its three components together in position on the dresser, and nail and glue it to the side planks and top. Glue and clamp the cross-halving joints.

If you have insufficient room in your workshop to finish the frieze with the dresser horizontal, glue and clamp the frieze only and tack them temporarily to the dresser. Slip some cling film or newspaper behind the cross-halving joints to prevent surplus glue bonding the frieze to the top plank (Fig. 10). When the glue is dry, remove the frieze and cut the remainder of the frieze.

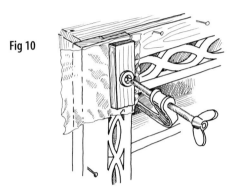

Fig 10

Sandpaper the edges of the pierced work and relieve some of the shapes with a chisel to add a little life to the work (see Special Skills, page 119).

Fit the additional strips to the front edge of the worktop, and the endboards, and glue them in place, holding them with masking or parcel tape (Fig. 11).

Fig 11

Make a template for the endboards of the worktop and saw them out with the jigsaw. Then sand the dresser.

7   Make up five lengths of square-section strip, a
    fraction under ⅜in (10mm) square, and tack these
    along the shelves close to the back to support
    dishes. Hold the strip with glue and veneer pins.

    Tack a length of square or half-round moulding
around the top of the dresser, setting it just above the
frieze and mitring the joints at the corners (Fig. 12).

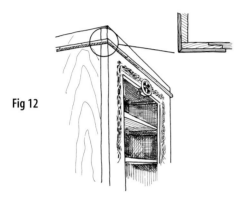

Fig 12

    Plane the two 45 degree bevels on the top and
bottom edges of the cornice to complete the
shaping of the cornice moulding, and cut out and
fit the cornice.

8   Nail some drawer runners inside the dresser,
    including a wide runner to support both drawers in
    the middle (Fig. 13).

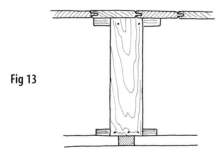

Fig 13

    Nail the runners at the side against the centre
batten, which should be in the ideal location for
this. If it is not, make up a wide runner, and screw
it to the sides, and support it at the back with a
wood block (Fig. 14).

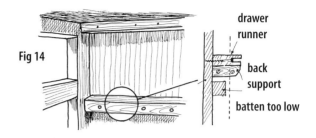

Fig 14

drawer
runner

back
support

batten too low

    Use a set square to mark in the position of the
drawer guides, and glue and tack them in place
(Fig. 15).

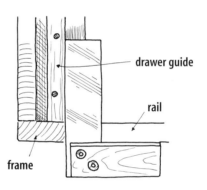

drawer guide

rail

frame

Fig 15

guide

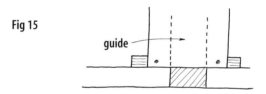

9   Make up two drawers to fit the dresser.

10 Make up the panelled doors and fit them. The door
    has a grooved doorframe with through mortise and
    tenon joints. Each tenon has a square haunch on its
    outer edge. Instructions for making the joints are
    on page 65 and those for fitting the panels are on
    page 68.

    Hang the doors, and fit drawer stops. Fit the key
escutcheons in the two drawers (see Special Skills,
page 122) and the brass knobs in the positions
indicated in the plans.

FINISHING

After filling the nail holes and sanding the dresser, I mixed a thin paint using burnt sienna pigment and water, with PVA glue as a binder. This was brushed on quickly with a 2in (50mm) brush and left to dry. The filler and some areas on the sides required some touching in later, with a slightly thicker mixture of paint and a watercolour brush.

After sanding down with 240 grit paper, I brushed on two coats of brown shellac floor sealer, and wiped it down with 0000 wire wool when it was completely dry. The dresser needed one coat of brown hard wax applied with a brush to finish.

TIP

When you are cutting out the pattern on the frieze, bore a hole through each pierced part of the pattern. Poke the jigsaw blade through the hole and start cutting from there (Fig. 16).

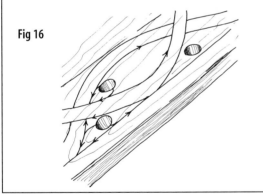

Fig 16

SPECIAL SKILLS

CUTTING A CROSS-HALVING JOINT

The two halving joints used in this book are illustrated in Figs. 17 and 18. The simple crossed joint is used in the front framework of the dresser, and the corner joint is used at the tops of the frieze. Without glue, these joints have no mechanical strength.

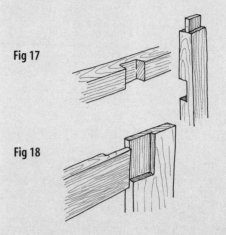

Fig 17

Fig 18

Place the pieces to be joined in position and mark the four shoulders with a knife. Just a slight nick on the corner is all that is required. Square across the shoulders with a knife and set square and square down the sides. When you are marking out cuts, prick the wood with the point of a knife.

Set a cutting or marking gauge to half the thickness of the pieces being joined if they are of equal thickness; if they are not, mark the appropriate depth that you want the joining piece sunk. Scribe the depth marks and shade in the waste areas (Fig. 19).

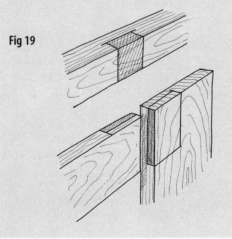

Fig 19

Use a tenon or dovetail saw to cut down the shoulders and, if the wood is hard or the cross-halving is a long one, make some additional cross-grain cuts to weaken the waste wood. Remove the waste with a sharp bevel-edge chisel (Fig. 20). Assemble the joint. Corrections are easy to make, but try to make the corrections in one go if you can; the joint loosens each time it is dismantled.

Cut the corner joint in a slightly different way. Marking out is much the same, except that because the joint is at a corner, you can use the marking gauge on more sides.

Cut the halving joint in the horizontal member either as you would a tenon or by sawing down the shoulder and chiselling out the waste with a broad sharp chisel. In the vertical, make three angled saw cuts (Fig. 21). Lay the joint face down and deepen the across-the-grain saw cuts with a mallet and chisel; the other you can leave because the wood will probably split along the scribe line. Work from the end and carefully split out the waste. Clean up the joint with a chisel.

Fig 20

Fig 21

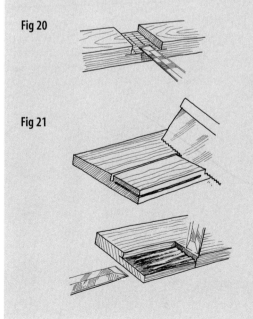

RELIEF CARVING THE FRIEZE

You do not have to do this, but in the simple frieze illustrated, the slight relief carving that has been applied strengthens the lines quite dramatically.

All you have to do is to incise the line to the depth of about $\frac{1}{8}$in (2mm), and shave away the wood to one side of the line. Where you can, hold the knife slightly at an angle so that the resulting edge is slightly more than 90 degrees (Fig. 22). This gives visual strength to the relief work. Never undercut the pattern – it looks messy.

After carving the frieze, sand it carefully. You do not need to round off the edges, but a light sanding helps to unify the work.

Fig 22

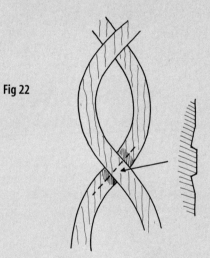

GRAVING OR PATCHING A PLANK

It is useful to be able to repair a plank with an almost invisible graving piece, but you should remember that a patch of any size will weaken the wood. The side of the dresser can have innumerable patches but a patch in the backrest of a chair might cause it to snap.

If you are using low-grade deal you are likely to

discover hidden pockets of resin, oozing sticky syrup. You cannot stop it, and you never know how much more there is to come out. The best thing to do is to cut it out and insert a patch.

There are other reasons for patching. You can conceal a mistake or, if you are using recycled wood, a patch can hide an earlier nail hole or joint.

Choose an offcut of similar wood, and hold it alongside the blemish, with its grain aligned to the grain on the plank. Sketch on the offcut the outline of the patch. Patches are usually diamond shaped, but whatever shape you choose, it should be large enough to cover the fault, have flat sides, and no corners of less than 45 degrees.

Saw out the patch using a dovetail saw, angling each side inwards by a degree or so. Hold the patch in position and slice around its outline with a sharp knife (Fig. 23).

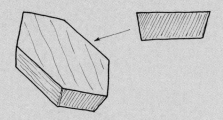

Fig 23

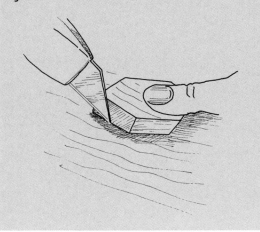

Take a $\frac{1}{4}$in (6mm) bevel-edge chisel and lightly cut out the centre of the area, first defining the area by a series of vertical cuts $\frac{1}{8}$in (2mm) inside the finished line (Fig. 24).

Fig 24

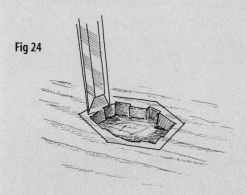

When the recess is deep enough, take a $\frac{3}{8}$in (10mm) chisel and cut back to the incised line. The final shavings are best started with the blade edge actually resting in the knife incision. Hold the graving piece in position to make sure it will fit, and if all is well, glue it and tap it in place.

Two-part resin glues are ideal for gluing patches as they set without the need for air. Keep a small pack of epoxy resin handy for this kind of repair work. Plane it level when the glue has cured.

FITTING THE CORNICE

If this cornice were made from a solid section of wood, measuring and marking the mitres would be simple. French provincial furniture is often capped with immensely heavy, solid cornice mouldings and fitting is easy. All you need do is measure from the corner of the dresser to the back vertical edge of the moulding. Square up with a set square and, when you get to the top, strike off an angle of 45 degrees and cut it.

For this cornice you will need 1in (25mm) panel

pins, glue and masking tape. You will also require a temporary bracket to hold the front moulding at the correct angle (Fig. 25).

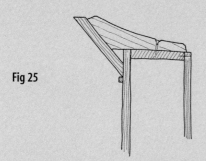

Fig 25

Marking the mitres on this lightweight cornice is no more difficult, but here are one or two tricks to help.

Mark off the exact position for the bottom edge of the cornice and tack a light square batten along the line to support the cornice. If your bead moulding, which is already in place, is high enough, that will do instead.

Lift up the cornice and tack it in place with a few half-driven panel pins. The long middle section of the cornice is fitted first, so line one end up (with about 6in (150mm) overhang at the side), which will be cut first. Fit the cornice support, which overhangs the top of the dresser, and nail it to the top, close to one of the front corners and clamp the cornice to it with a G-clamp.

Pencil on the back edge of the cornice the position of the corner of the dresser. This line is perpendicular and you are pencilling on one of the bevels worked earlier (Fig. 26).

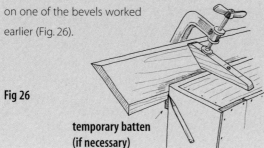

Fig 26

temporary batten (if necessary)

Remove the cornice. Stick the end of a plank upright in the vice and check that it is perpendicular to the vice jaws and no higher than the cornice when it is held at its correct angle against it. Hold the cornice there, with the mitre square mark in the line of the mitre on the top bevel (Fig. 27).

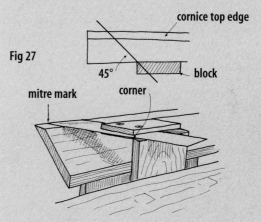

Fig 27

cornice top edge

45° **block**

mitre mark **corner**

Remove the cornice moulding, and connect the two lines with a ruler. This gives you the line to cut. Clamp the cornice against the plank or tilt it in the vice, and saw it. Trim with a shoulder plane.

Replace the cornice on the dresser and tack it there. Clamp the top edge as before. Your cut should lead directly from the front corner of the dresser.

Mark the other end in the same way and saw it off. Cut a little on the waste side of the line and trim the mitre with a shoulder plane.

Take a sliding bevel and record the mitre angle at the front of the cornice. It might be useful when marking out the returns (Fig. 28).

Fig 28

Once the front piece is in position, the returns can almost be marked off by eye and planed until they fit. This is not as tricky or as risky as it sounds – if you cut the remaining cornice moulding in half you should have ample left for adjustment.

Hold the return in place and use a parallel offcut of card to mark the angle at the top. Sight down the front mitre to give you a rough line for the vertical cut (Fig. 29). Check it against the sliding bevel setting – they should be about the same angle, but if they are not, sight it again with the card, before sawing it off. Lift the return into position and see if it fits. If it does, you have saved yourself a lot of trouble. If it does not,

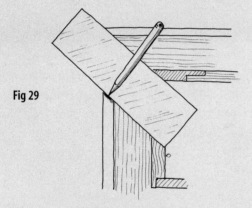

Fig 29

adjust the angles with a plane until they do.

When your first return fits, glue and nail it to the dresser. Do not glue the mitre join, but hold the corner together with masking tape.

Fit the other return and glue it.

Lastly, remove the main length of cornice moulding and apply glue to the surface nailed to the dresser and to the mitres. Lift it back up and pin it back in place. With luck, your pins will slip into their previous holes, making positioning easy.

Hold the mitres with masking tape (Fig. 30). When the glue has dried, remove the tape and carve some wood blocks to slip behind the mitres. Fit them with lots of glue.

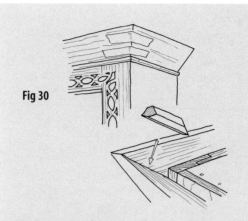

Fig 30

SINKING ESCUTCHEONS

Simple escutcheons, which are recessed into the drawer or door front, can be bought from most ironmongers. Some are split and press together once they are tapped into position. Better quality escutcheons are cast and are easier to fit.

Pencil in the position for each escutcheon. Drill a $\frac{1}{4}$in (6mm) diameter hole to start off the excavation required to fit it. Take the escutcheon in a pair of long-nosed pliers, hold it in position and give it a sharp tap with a hammer. This should indent the outline of its flange (Fig. 31).

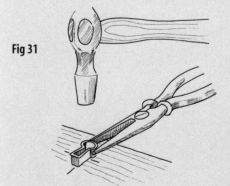

Fig 31

Cut to this line with some thin, sharp chisels. Make sure that the recess you dig is deep enough to sink the entire escutcheon flush with the wood surface. When you think you are about ready, hammer it into place.

CUTTING LIST
Kitchen Dresser (nominal sizes: in/mm)

Item	Quantity	Length	Width	Thickness
Sides	2	84/2134	10/255	1/25 Fir
	2	40/1016	10/255	1/25
Front				
Stiles	2	32/815	2/50	1³/₄/45
Centre	1	29/735	2/50	1³/₄/45
Rails	2	44/1120	2/50	1³/₄/45
	1	44/1120	1³/₄/45	1³/₄/45
Worktop	2	44/1120	10/255	1/25
Cup floor	2	44/1120	10/255	1/25
Shelves	5	44/1120	10/255	1/25
Frieze	1	44/1120	6/150	1/25
	2	51/1300	6/150	1/25
Cornice	1	76/1930	4/100	³/₄/19
Doors				
Stiles	4	11/280	4/100	1/25
Rails	4	19¹/₂/495	4/100	1/25
Panels	4	11/280	7/178	1/25
Drawers				
Front	2	19¹/₂/495	7/178	1¹/₄/32
Sides	4	12/305	7/178	³/₄/19
Back	2	19/485	6/150	³/₄/19
Battens	7	18/457	1/25	1/25

Drawer bottoms: plywood ¹/₄in (6mm) offcuts

Drawer runners and guides: workshop offcuts

Back: tongue and groove to make panel 80 x 44 x ³/₄in (2030 x 1120 x 19mm)

1in grid

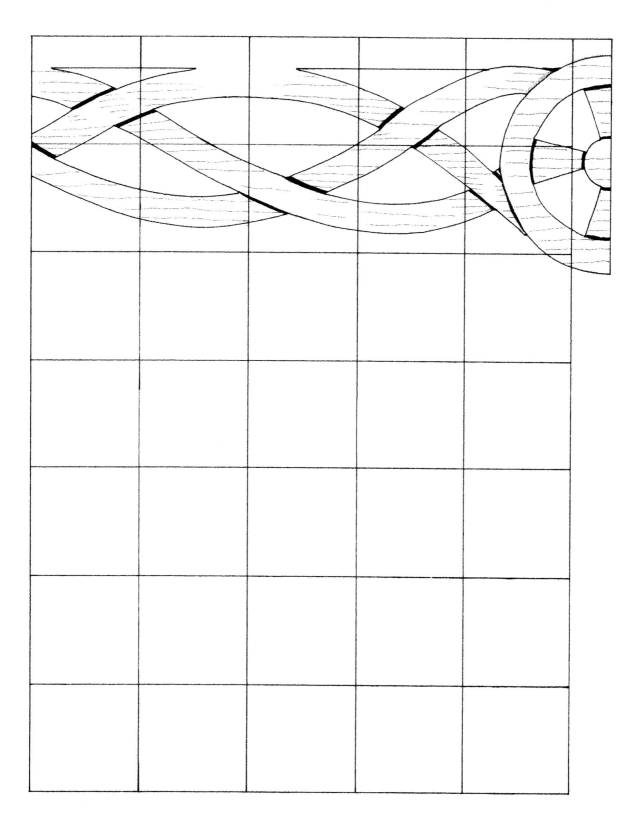

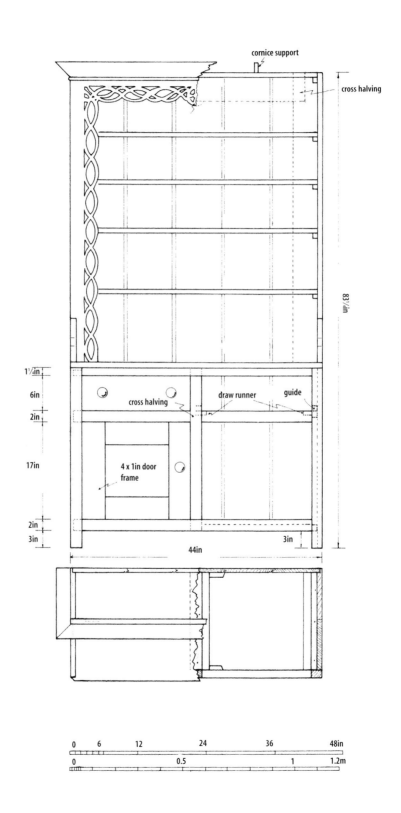

cornice support

cross halving

83¾in

1¼in

6in

cross halving

draw runner

guide

2in

17in

4 x 1in door frame

2in

3in

3in

44in

| 0 | 6 | 12 | | 24 | 36 | 48in |
| 0 | | | 0.5 | | 1 | 1.2m |

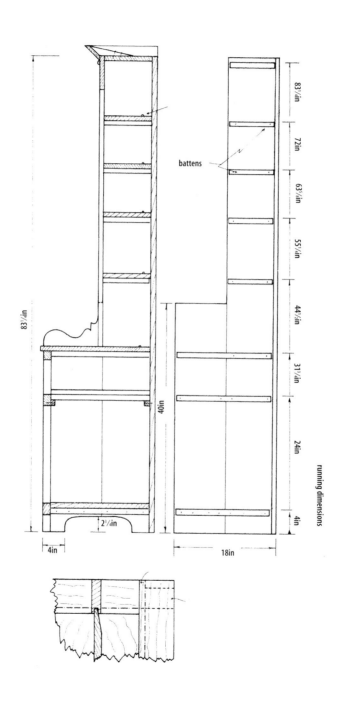

83¼in

83¼in

72in

63¾in

battens

55¼in

44½in

40in

31½in

24in

running dimensions

4in

2¼in

4in

18in

CUPBOARD OFFICE

This cupboard has a specific purpose. It is designed to contain all the bills, letters, files, ledgers and notebooks that home workers leave scattered about. It is made deep enough to hold a computer and large printer, and it is also big enough to hold a wide-screen television

and hundreds of videos and audio tapes. When it is used as a desk, it has a slide at table height for a keyboard or typewriter, and inside are mounted a bank of power points and an overhead spotlight.

The design is based on an early twentieth-century two-door pine cupboard, but the sides have been made a little deeper to accommodate office machinery. With the growing trend of people working from home, it is useful to have a work unit like this. It allows for efficient organisation and, when the door is closed, its appearance is in keeping with even the prettiest of country cottages.

METHOD

1 Select the boards for the sides, top, bottom and shelves. Work a shallow rebate in the back edge plank of each side, glue the sides together and hold them with clamps and nailed battens.

Make up the top and bottom boards. They extend the full width of the cupboard, and are narrower than the sides by the depth of the rebate in the back (Fig. 1).

Fig 1

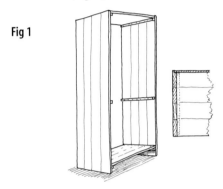

Because the doors are made from wider wood than the front framework, the centre shelf is 1½in (38mm) narrower. This gives clearance for the doorframe, and leaves room for the front of the slide.

The width is made up by a couple of ear pieces glued at the front corners of the shelf (Fig. 2).

Once the top and bottom and shelves have been glued, plane them flat and sand them smooth using a rough belt in a belt sander. Trim them all to the same length with a handsaw.

Fig 2

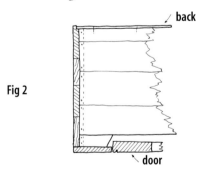

back

door

2 Glue and nail the bottom plank onto the bottom batten on one side. Support the joint at right angles

with a diagonal batten nailed to the front edge (see Tip, page 42). Glue and nail the second side and support this, too. Fit the centre shelf, and nail and glue it down. Fit and fasten the top.

Lower the box onto two trestles, face down. Sight across the edges to make certain they are all parallel. If they are not, correct the heights of the trestles until they are. Check the diagonals and correct any errors. Once the back is nailed in place, these kind of faults are difficult to eliminate (Fig. 3).

Fig 3

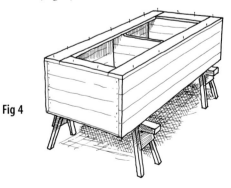

3 Measure the carcass and cut the ¼in (6mm) plywood sheet to size. Nail it into the rebate, remembering to mark the position of the centre shelf. Use 1in (25mm) wire nails to secure the back.

Put the carcass to one side, and make the simple mortised doorframe. Take its overall dimensions from the carcass, not the drawings, glue the framework together and nail it onto the front of the carcass (Fig. 4).

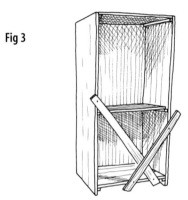

Fig 4

4   The doors are made to fit the framework. Notice that they have a simple bead moulding worked on the outside of the stiles and the inside of the rails. Cut the stile mouldings when fitted (Fig. 5).

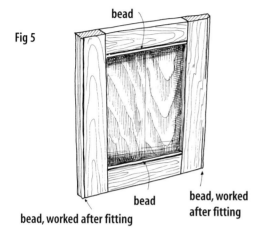

Fig 5

bead

bead

bead, worked after fitting

bead, worked after fitting

bead, worked after fitting

The tenons are haunched to fill the groove; for advice on making these doors see page 133, and for hanging them see page 47.

Hang the bottom door first, and then fit, glue and screw the false division to its top.

Slip a couple of sheets of card onto the top of the lower door before fitting the top door to provide adequate clearance.

5   Nail together the simple guides and runners that hold the slide (Fig. 6). Mark their position. Notice that the slide is positioned so that it misses the doors when then are opened at right angles to the front of the cupboard (Fig. 7). Clamp the guides in place and secure them with screws driven from above.

6   Make up the slide. At each end of the slide is a wooden strip, called a clamp, which prevents it from warping. It is glued and held to the edges with a feather tongue (Fig. 8).

First, glue the main surface of transverse planks together, butt joining them. When they are dry, trim the ends and work a groove down each side.

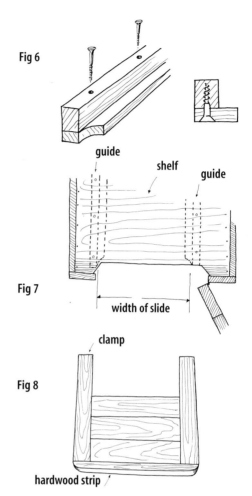

Fig 6

guide

shelf

guide

Fig 7

width of slide

clamp

Fig 8

hardwood strip

As long as you arrange a suitable support to hold the plank vertical, you can cut the groove with the circular saw. Alternatively, cut it with a router, plough plane or biscuit jointer.

Make a similar groove in the clamps, and then saw a hardwood tongue to fit in the groove (Fig. 9). Glue and clamp the slide together.

Plane the top level and glue on the hardwood front edge. Trim the slide until it moves easily beneath the centre shelf.

7   Make up the pigeon holes from the left-over plywood (Figs. 10 and 11), and fit the shelves (Fig. 12). The file boxes beneath the bottom shelf are just nailed together (Fig. 13).

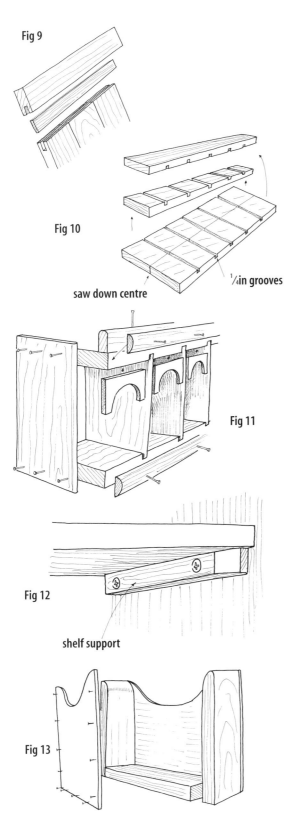

Fig 9

Fig 10

saw down centre

¼in grooves

Fig 11

Fig 12

shelf support

Fig 13

WIRING

I fitted a spotlight in the top left-hand corner and wired two switches into the cupboard. One household switch is mounted on the inside of the doorframe, and can be used to switch on the light when the door is opened. A second switch, which breaks the circuit automatically when the door is closed, is screwed to the underside of the slide guide.

I also wired in a 13 amp socket and switch below the main shelf into which a panel of sockets can be connected. A hole, 1in (25mm) in diameter, was drilled through the back shelf to carry all the cables. The power and light are supplied by an earthed cable passing through the side of the cupboard and leading to a 13 amp plug, fitted with a low amp fuse.

FINISHING

I stained the cupboard with a mixture of Canadian cedar, English light oak and American walnut Colron stains. When it was dry, I applied four brushed coats of button polish, followed by wax. For the inside, I made up a matt blue paint using blue, green and black powder pigments, with PVA glue as a binder.

TIP

If you want to mark out an accurate right angle on a large scale, construct a 345 triangle. Take a large pair of dividers, strike off 5 units on a straight batten and number them. Mark off 4 units from the corner along one straight side. Mark off 3 more or less at right angles to the side from the corner. Hold the zero end of the stick at the 4 mark on the side, point the stick towards the 3. Where the 5 and the 3 meet, make a mark and connect it to the corner. This line will be at right angles to the side.

SPECIAL SKILL

MAKING A DOOR

The framework of this cupboard door is joined with through tenons. This is appropriate because the doors are heavy and the broad through tenons provide the maximum possible glued area to support the weight. An additional benefit of the through tenon is that, because it is cut from both sides, the joint is likely to be true.

Cut all the pieces for the frame. Mark the face sides and face edges. Work the mouldings and the ³⁄₈ in (10mm) groove on the inside edges.

With the rails laid over the stiles, mark the positions for the shoulders (Fig. 14). Incise the shoulder lines around the rails with a knife and set square and mark off the positions for the rails on the stiles.

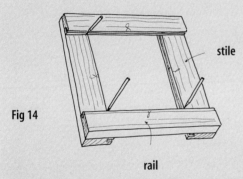

Fig 14

stile

rail

Cut away the waste on the inside edges of the tenons – that is, the two sides of the groove (Fig. 15).

Set the mortise gauge against a ³⁄₈ in (10mm) chisel and mark both the mortises and tenons (Fig. 16). Saw the tenons (see page 66) and trim their shoulders with a rebate plane. Do not cut beyond the shoulder line.

Use a marking gauge to scribe in the haunches at the outside edges of the tenons. Use a slip of wood the exact depth of the groove to mark the depth of the haunch.

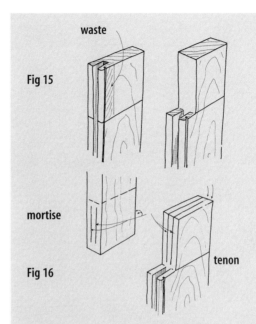

waste

Fig 15

mortise

Fig 16

tenon

Number the tenons, and then lay them, one at a time, against the stiles, and pencil in the length and position of each mortise and the number of the joint (Fig. 17).

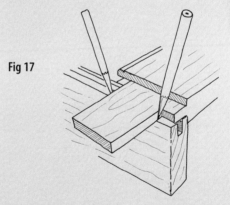

Fig 17

Transfer the mortise marks to the outside of the stiles (Fig. 18). Use the mortise gauge to scribe the mortises, bearing the gauge against the face side of the stile.

Cut out the mortise, starting in the groove and working to the centre of the stile. Finish the mortise on the inside with vertical cuts, then turn the stile over and work towards the centre from the outside.

CUTTING LIST

Cupboard Office (nominal sizes: in/mm)

Item	Quantity	Length	Width	Thickness
Side planks	8	75/1905	10/255	1/25
Top and bottom	8	36/915	10/255	1/25
Front frame				
Sides	2	75/1905	5/127	1/25
Top and bottom	2	36/915	5/127	1/25
Shelves				
Centre	4	36/915	10/255	1/25
Others	4	36/915	10/255	1/25
	1	48/1220	10/255	1/25
Doors				
Top stiles	2	33/838	5/127	$1\frac{1}{4}$/32
Top rails	2	27/685	5/127	$1\frac{1}{4}$/32
Bottom stiles	2	32/815	5/127	$1\frac{1}{4}$/32
	2	27/685	5/127	$1\frac{1}{4}$/32
Decorative rail	1	27/685	$1\frac{1}{4}$/32	$1\frac{1}{4}$/32
Panels				
Top	2	26/660	10/255	1/25
Bottom	2	$24\frac{1}{2}$/622	10/255	1/25
Slide	2	22/558	3/75	1/25
	3	22/510	5/127	$\frac{3}{4}$/19
Hardwood strip	1	26/660	1/25	1/25 Oak
Runners	2	24/610	$1\frac{1}{4}$/32	$1\frac{1}{4}$/32
	2	24/610	2/50	1/25
Battening	6	24/610	1/25	1/25
	8	15/380	1/25	1/25
Plywood back	1	75/1905	36/915	$\frac{1}{4}$/6 Low grade

Pigeonholes and files: made from offcuts

All items are fir unless otherwise indicated

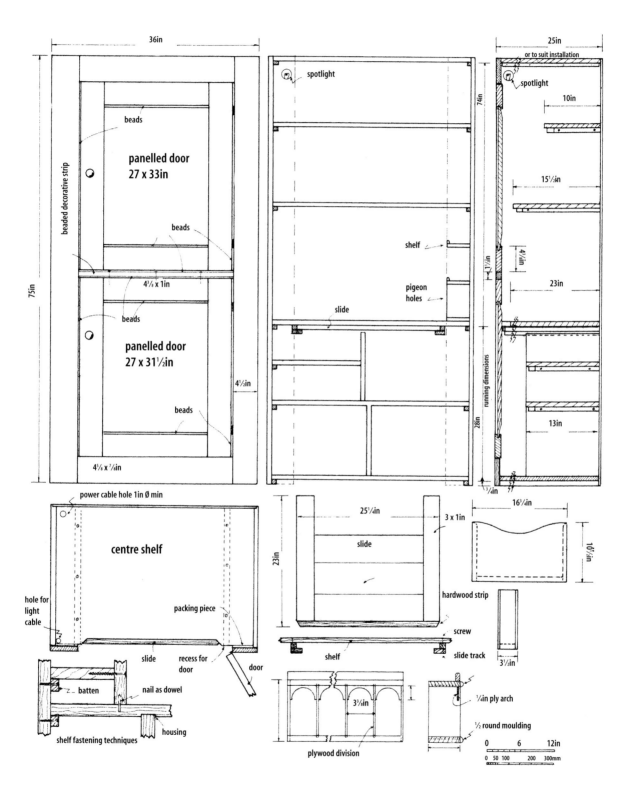

36in

beaded decorative strip

beads

panelled door
27 x 33in

beads

$4^7/_8$ x 1in

beads

panelled door
27 x 31½in

$4^5/_8$ x $^7/_8$in

75in

$4^1/_2$in

beads

spotlight

shelf

pigeon
holes

slide

25in

or to suit installation

spotlight

10in

15½in

$4^7/_8$in

23in

13in

74in

1½in

28in

running dimensions

$3^1/_4$in

power cable hole 1in Ø min

centre shelf

hole for
light
cable

slide

packing piece

recess for
door

door

batten

nail as dowel

shelf fastening techniques

housing

23in

25¼in

slide

3 x 1in

shelf

screw

slide track

$3^1/_8$in

hardwood strip

16¾in

10½in

$3^3/_8$in

plywood division

¼in ply arch

½ round moulding

0   6   12in

0 50 100   200   300mm

135

TWELVE-DRAWER CHEST

The only joints that might cause a problem in this small chest are the dovetails at the top corners. I have included a Special Skill, which describes cutting and fitting a keyed mitre joint. Instructions for cutting dovetails can be found in my book *Handbook of Furniture Restoration*. Alternatives are shown on the plans, and I have included appropriate instructions.

This pretty chest requires a lot of machine work. Before you start, check the parallel guide on your circular saw. If there is any movement at all in its setting once it is clamped, make arrangements to correct it.

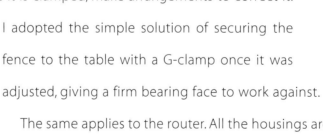

I adopted the simple solution of securing the fence to the table with a G-clamp once it was adjusted, giving a firm bearing face to work against.

The same applies to the router. All the housings are cut with the router, and it is worth taking the trouble to make substantial templates that are easy to use.

METHOD

1 The carcass of the chest is made first. Plough or saw the rebates in the planks to hold the back.

Mark and cut the sides and top, shelves and bottom to length. Remember to add the ¼in (6mm) at each end of the shelves and bottom (Fig. 1) to fit into the housings.

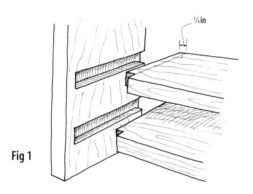

Fig 1

2 Clamp the two ends together and use a sharp pencil to mark off the shoulders for the top and bottom and the two shelves. Square across the inside faces.

Cut the joints at the top corners (see Special Skills, page 142).

3 The shelves, bottom and vertical divisions are fitted into stopped housings. Fig. 2 shows this simple joint, and you will see that the ends entering the housings are notched at the front and the housings are stopped short of the front edge.

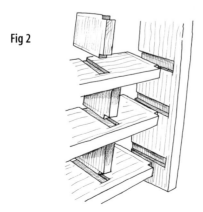

Fig 2

Mark out all the housings with a knife, clamping the sides together and the shelves together to be certain that they will be in line. Avoid running the scribe lines onto the corner of the front edges, where they would be seen.

Make a template to use with the guide plate on the router. It is much easier to locate the template in position, if it incorporates its own fence (Fig. 3).

Rout out the stopped housings, wearing ear defenders and proper safety goggles. Ordinary plastic spectacle lenses give inadequate protection. Vacuum up the mess.

Chisel square the front corners of the housings.

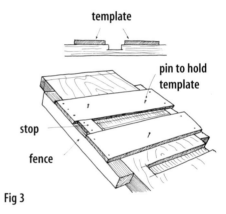

Fig 3

4 Clamp the top, the two shelves and the bottom together. At each end, transfer the shoulder line of the top right across the other three planks. Incise this line with a knife (Fig. 4).

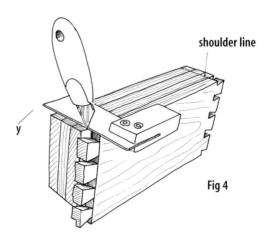

Fig 4

138

Separate the pieces and square back from the edges. Set the marking gauge to the distance 'y' and scribe across the end of the notches. Cut out the notches using a dovetail saw.

Although these are simple little notches, any mistakes you make will be difficult to conceal. There are two simple and effective tricks you might adopt here. First, make the saw cut ½in (0.5mm) on the waste side of the line, and trim back with a sharp chisel; alternatively, relieve the line with a chisel and lodge the saw in the groove before cutting. This method, which is described on page 11, is the quicker of the two and the one I would use.

5   Check that all the joints fit, then glue and assemble the carcass, driving ovals or lost heads into the ends of the shelves. Do not leave the carcass to dry until you have checked the diagonals and left it square.

Once the glue has dried, run glue into the housings and slide the shelves and partitions into place.

6   The bracket feet are mitred as shown in Fig. 5. Cut the feet from the end of a long board, saw them to shape and mark out the mitres. Saw the mitres once the shaping is complete.

They are mitred into the sides. Turn the cabinet over, mark off the 45 degree mitre and carefully saw down the corner. If you are worried about doing this, saw on the waste side and trim the cut with a chisel (see page 119).

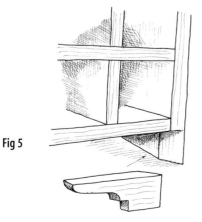

Fig 5

If you end up with an angle of less than 45 degrees, don't worry. A glue block will hide the mistake.

7   Cut out and fasten the back board into position.

8   Select wood for the sides, back and fronts of the drawers (Fig. 6). Do not cut them to length at this stage, but saw them into strips, each a little too wide to fit into their openings, and each long enough to make a row of components – that is, four drawer fronts, eight drawer sides and four drawer backs.

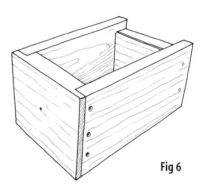

Fig 6

Identify each strip to avoid confusion and stack them together in three groups, one for each row of drawers.

Set the circular saw and cut the grooves in the front and side strips. The back is not grooved; it sits on top of the drawer bottom.

9   Number off the drawer openings, writing their numbers in pencil on the rails. Fit the fronts first. This is easy but time consuming. Concentrate on one horizontal row at a time because these drawers at least should be all the same height. Plane the top until the ends can be poked into their drawer openings (Fig. 7). If your planing is reasonably good, it is likely that the inside drawers will also fit.

Hold the end of the strip across the entrance to the first drawer. Trim the end until it sits parallel to

Fig 7

the side of the chest and pencil in the mark for the opposite side. Square this round in pencil and saw it off just on the waste side. Trim the new edge to fit, using a shoulder plane and shooting board. Repeat with the rest of the drawers on the top row. Repeat for the lower rows. Number each drawer on the inside as you fit it, and remember that the groove is at the bottom of the drawer.

Set the circular saw, try out your saw settings on a scrap of waste and then cut the lap joints in the edges of the drawers (Fig. 8).

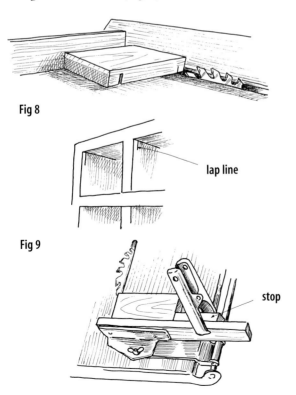

Fig 8

lap line

Fig 9

stop

10 Fit the drawer sides, working in the same order. If you scribe a gauge line on the front rail to show the length of the lap required, you can cut them to the right length using the angle guide on the circular saw (Fig. 9).

The height of the backs is not critical. Bevel the top edges, and cut them to length, equal to the distance between the shoulders of the drawer.

While the saw is set up for mass production, saw out the drawer bottoms, making them a fraction wider than necessary. Plane them to fit later.

11 Assemble each drawer without glue, holding it with a thick rubber band. Dismantle and glue the drawers together one at a time. Spread glue onto both faces of the lap joint. Hold the front and one side together, and slip the drawer bottom into the groove. Lodge it in the vice, with the front resting on a scrap of wood laid across the bars. Nail the first side in place (Fig. 10).

Fig 10

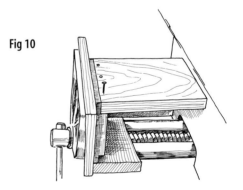

Insert a suitably sized steadying piece into the drawer and nail the back to the side (Fig. 11). Put the drawer back in the vice, leaving the steadying piece inside, and glue and nail the opposite side.

Check the drawer to see if it is square, correcting it if necessary, before nailing on the bottom with panel pins.

Repeat with all the other drawers.

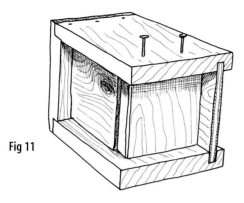

Fig 11

12   When the glue is dry, refit the drawers. They are not likely to fit without adjustment. Punch down any nail heads before planing.

    Drill the holes for the knobs with a bradawl, fill blemishes with two-part hard wood filler, then slide in the drawers and sand the front smooth. Finish with 240 grit paper.

FINISHING

I stained this little chest with aniline stains, which are soluble in methylated spirits but are not light fast, although a degree of fading is quite acceptable. Mix the stains by adding a few aniline crystals to about a quarter of a cupful of methylated spirits or finishing spirit. Stir the mixture well, test it and, if it is strong enough, strain it into another bottle.

    Wipe the stain over the carcass using a mop of cotton wool, wrapped up in a clean cotton rag and leave it to dry.

    When you have finished staining, add some transparent shellac polish to each stain and apply this thin polish with a brush or a mop. Repeat several times, allowing plenty of drying time between coats, until the chest has a good finish.

    Apply a couple more coats of unthinned transparent polish to the carcass and drawers and leave them to dry. Rub down the chest with 000 wire wool and wax it.

TIPS

• When making right-angled saw cuts, use the angle guide. Run a few test pieces before making the cuts, and if you find it difficult to align the wood to the blade, stick a strip of masking tape across the saw table, on the feed side, and mark on it the exact line of the cut (Fig. 12).

Fig 12

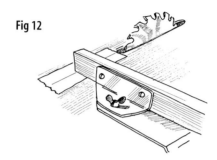

• When you are paring and trimming on small areas, a sharp chisel used with its bevel up is the best tool for smoothing uneven surfaces such as these. (Sometimes a steel sandplate backed by a flat wooden block will do the trick.)

• For planing fine shavings or end grain, move the cap iron down until it is set just behind the sharp-edged blade.

SPECIAL SKILLS

SHOOTING BOARD

The shooting board illustrated in Fig. 13 is a convenient size to have in the workshop. It can be used for shooting edge joints up to 15in (380mm) long and also for trimming end grain, when its endstop will prevent splitting.

Fig 13

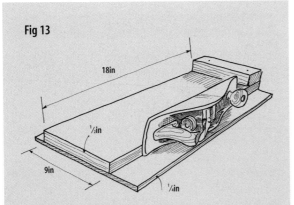

Press the piece of wood you are shooting against the endstop. The plane is held on its side and slipped along the bottom plywood strip. This controls its line and guarantees that the plane sole is vertical. Rub candlewax on the strip.

When it is in use the board can be screwed to the bench or lodged against the bench stop.

Plane blades are usually sharpened to a slight curve, so it is important to adjust the tilt of the blade to suit the height of the piece of wood you are planing. The angle of the blade can be adjusted by manipulating the lever just above the handle.

MITRED AND KEYED JOINT

The holding power in a plain mitre joint comes from the glue, and any additional glue blocks, nails or screws that have been used. Without a mechanical element to the joint it is not suitable for carcass making. A simple way of providing some mechanical strength is to insert keys of thin wood at angles across the mitre (Fig. 14).

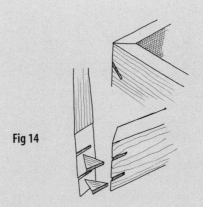

Fig 14

Marking and Cutting the Mitres

Mitres have to be marked accurately, because errors seem to multiply if they are badly marked or poorly cut. If these are the first mitres you have attempted, add a couple of inches for adjustment to each side and to the top piece before you begin to saw and trim.

Use a sharp hard pencil for marking. Square across on the outside face and use the mitre square to strike off the 45 degree marks. Hold the workpiece in the vice and saw just to the waste of the pencil line with a cross-cut handsaw (Fig. 15).

Fig 15

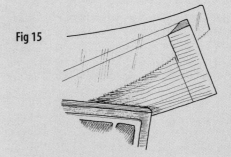

This is quite a long cut, and it is likely that your saw will veer off line. As long as it veers to the waste side you need not worry because the surplus can be removed by plane later. If you begin to cut into the line, stop and begin again from the other end.

Hold the plank in the vice (Fig. 16) and slowly plane the mitre flat. The blade has to be very sharp, and you must press the sole hard against the sawn face of the mitre. Lubricate the sole with candlewax to help ease its movement.

Fig 16

Once the mitre is trimmed, check that it is quite flat. Retract the blade of a larger plane and press the planed surface against its sole. Trim away any high spots.

Saw and plane the counterpart and hold the two pieces together. Check that the angle they make is 90 degrees and that the joint is closed up. If they do not make 90 degrees, one or both of the faces will have to be adjusted. As before, this is done with the shoulder plane, and you must remember to take advantage of the slight curve of the blade by taking the thicker shavings with the centre of the blade and finer ones at the edge (see page 14).

When the mitres are ready, they can be glued together. Draw the teeth of a hacksaw across both surfaces to roughen them, and improve the grip of the glue. Place the joint as shown in Fig. 17 and strap it tightly with parcel tape. Turn over the pieces, run glue in the joint and pull it closed. Wipe away surplus glue and hold it closed with tape.

Fig 17

Fitting the Keys

The keys are inserted after the glue has dried. Hold the joint in the vice, and use a handsaw to make $\frac{1}{16}$ in (1mm) wide incisions across the joint (Fig. 18).

Fig 18

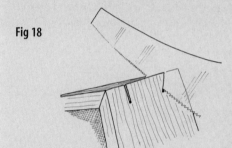

Cut some straight-grained slices of wood, run glue into the cuts and tap the wood home. You will find that if you plane a fine taper over the length of the key, you will be able to tap it into position across the joint, where it will fit tightly (Fig. 19). When the glue has dried, trim the keys.

Fig 19

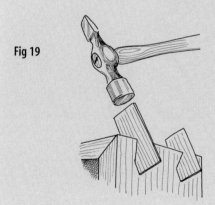

Alternatively, the slots can be cut with the circular saw. Adjust the height of the blade and the parallel fence to give you the cut you want, and arrange a stop so that the cut does not become too deep (Fig. 20).

Fig 20

A carbide-tipped combination blade will cut a clean, smooth-edged slot, about $\frac{1}{8}$ in (2mm) wide. So although the cuts will be square to the corner, rather than angled, there is ample strength in the keys to compensate for a slight loss of mechanical strength (Fig. 21).

Fig 21

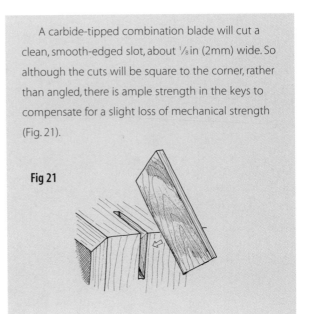

CUTTING LIST
Twelve-drawer Chest (nominal sizes: in/mm)

Item	Quantity	Length	Width	Thickness
Top	1	$17\frac{1}{4}$/440	7/178	$\frac{3}{4}$/19
Sides	2	$13\frac{1}{2}$/345	7/178	$\frac{3}{4}$/19
Shelves	3	17/430	7/178	$\frac{3}{4}$/19
Dividers	9	$3\frac{1}{2}$/89	7/178	$\frac{3}{4}$/19
Feet	2	$3\frac{1}{8}$/80	2/50	$\frac{3}{4}$/19
Drawers				
Fronts	12	$3\frac{3}{4}$/95	$3\frac{1}{2}$/89	1/25
Sides	24	6/150	$3\frac{1}{2}$/89	$\frac{3}{4}$/19
Backs	12	$2\frac{1}{2}$/64	3/75	$\frac{3}{4}$/19
Bottoms	12	6/150	3/75	$\frac{1}{4}$/6

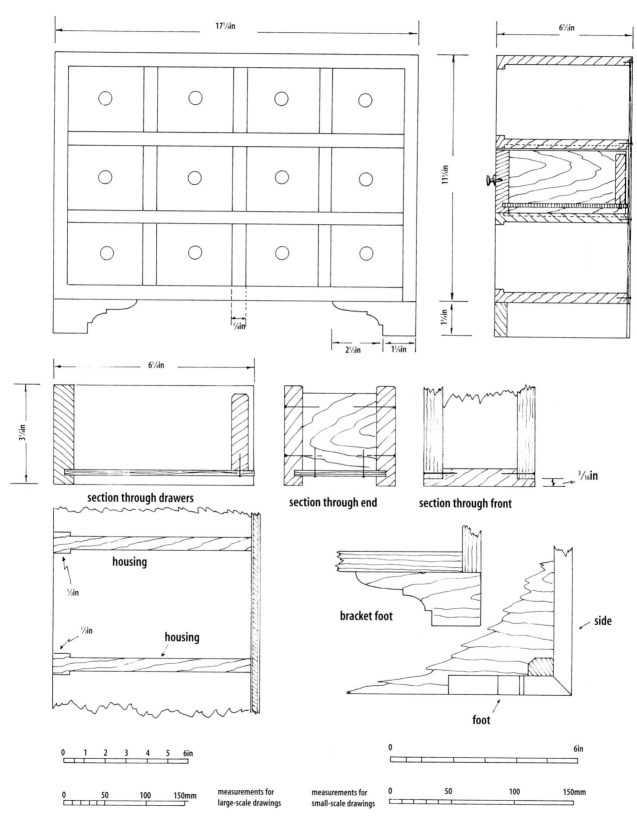

17¼in

6⅛in

11¾in

1¼in

⅝in

2½in   1⅝in

6¼in

3¼in

section through drawers

section through end

section through front

³⁄₁₆in

housing

⅛in

⅛in

housing

bracket foot

side

foot

0 1 2 3 4 5 6in

0   50   100   150mm

measurements for
large-scale drawings

measurements for
small-scale drawings

0   6in

0   50   100   150mm

145

TRESTLE TABLE

One of the advantages of a trestle table is that you can seat more people in comfort round it than you can a similar sized conventional table. Trestles are also much easier to make.

Their great disadvantage is that they tend to sway. To overcome this, joints and wood sections have to be substantial, so it is not often that you see a table with such a light and delicate construction.

This is a copy of a mid-seventeenth century American trestle table, which is made from oak, and comfortably seats eight people. A similar table to this, in the Henry Ford Museum at Dearborn, is fitted with diagonal supports to steady

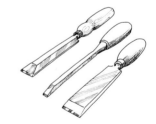

it. When I made this table, I also made the diagonals, but for reasons I describe in the following instructions, they have been unnecessary.

METHOD

This is an easy and inexpensive table to make. The top is joined with loose tenons and screwed to the base using metal stretcher plates. The subframe is stub-tenoned together, and the legs are screwed to the subframe with coach screws (Fig. 1). Decoration is provided by a bead worked on the corners of the verticals and the stretcher,

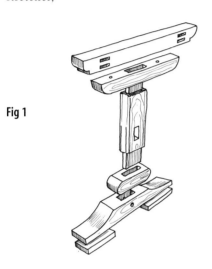

Fig 1

If you can, make the top from planks cut on the quarter. It is unlikely that you will be able to find many such quarter-sawn planks, however, so position your planks with the heartwood upwards, which will probably be the best way of keeping the timber flat. Store the planks in the house for a while, before planing the top planks smooth and shooting the edges. Join them together with loose tongues and sand them smooth.

1 Cut out the components for the subframe. Round off the ends of the two pieces that form the ends of the frame with either a bow saw or a jigsaw fitted with a T 244D curve-cutting blade. Finish the shaping with a file, or with 100 grit paper backed against an offcut of wood (Fig. 2).

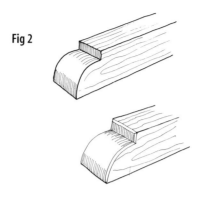

Fig 2

2 Mark out the joints, grouping the components in pairs. The shoulders of the tenons should be marked as a pair as should the positions for the mortises (Fig. 3). While you are marking the tenons and have the pieces clamped together, mark in the position for the two cross-braces. Cut the twin stub tenons at the ends of each side member and mark the mortises for them. If you only have one mortise gauge, set the gauge for the tenon closest to the face edge and mark all four mortises and tenons, and then reset it for the other four, and mark them (Fig. 4).

Fig 3

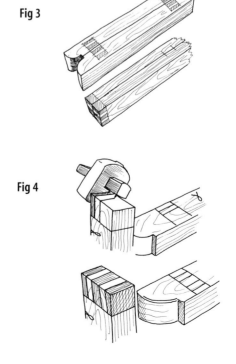

Fig 4

Cut the tenons, removing the waste between the tenons with a coping saw and chisel (Fig. 5). Chop out the mortises, cutting only to the depth of the tenons.

Fit the joints and cut and fit the cross-members.

Fig 5

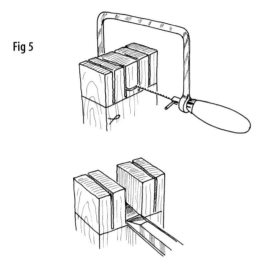

3   Make up the end trestles. These are tenoned at the ends and each vertical has a mortise to hold the stretcher. When you have made the legs, make and fit the stretcher and prepare to pull it tight with draw pegs (see page 88).

Once the joints are cut and fitted and the beads moulded, shape the ends of the trestle legs and supports. Glue the joints together.

4   The trestle legs are screwed to the underside of the subframe. Before doing this, attach the subframe to the underside of the top with stretcher plates (Fig. 6). It is much easier to do this without the legs in the way (see Special Skills, page 151).

Glue the stretcher to the two legs, and knock in the draw pegs, and then screw the legs to the subframe, using four 4in (100mm) coach screws, with a washer beneath each head (see Tip, page 150).

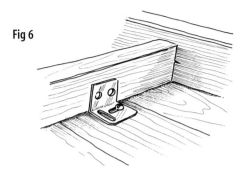

Fig 6

5   Because stretcher tables always seem to sway and wobble, I cut the long cross-stretcher ⅛in (6mm) too long. With tight-fitting tenons, pulled tight with a draw peg, and glued, it required some force to line up and fasten the leg assembly to the subframe. Because this tension inside the framework has provided additional stiffness, I dispensed with the diagonal brace supports. One day, though, it will probably need them.

Stand the table on its feet and leave it until the glue has hardened.

FINISHING

The table featured here was, like the oak chest, masked with brown sauce before being lightly fumed and then finished with wax. For advice on fuming and masking see page 86. The size of the table presented some problems for fuming. It is possible, with a table as large as this, to make a polythene bag and insert sufficient ammonia in dishes inside the bag to get an even coloration, but instead of doing this, I draped a thin sheet of polythene loosely over the table, and used weights to hold it to the floor. I used a fan heater – using only the fan facility – and taped the polythene to it, taking care not to block the air inlet. The heater was outside the polythene tent.

I placed a large dish with a cupful of ammonia in it in front of the fan and turned on the motor. Air inflated the tent, lifting the polythene from the surface of the table and circulating the ammonia

fumes. I left the table for about an hour before removing the polythene and washing off the masking sauce with methylated spirits.

When the table was dry and most of the smell had gone, I waxed it with a quick-drying black wax. I applied two heavy coats and then wiped down the top with coarse wire wool to remove all the surface accumulations of wax. I finished with two applications of a light brown 'antique' wax. When you are building up a wax finish, the secret is to apply the wax thinly and frequently. Too thick a layer will not harden and is easily marked.

TIPS

• When you are mortising and cutting stub tenons, check the depth of cut by gumming a slip of masking tape to the side of the chisel at the finished depth or dab a spot of white correction fluid on the blade at the full depth.

• Coach screws have great holding power, but you need to pre-drill to the full length of the screw. Drill a hole that is the full diameter of the shank. Then the threaded part must be pre-drilled with a drill bit smaller than the thread (Fig. 7). Tighten with a spanner. A washer beneath the square head will protect the wood.

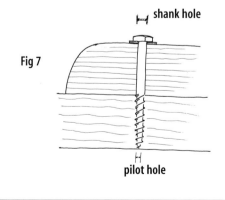

shank hole

Fig 7

pilot hole

SPECIAL SKILLS

FASTENING A STRETCHER PLATE

Stretcher plates are fastened with short, round-head screws. There are two faces, one of which is slotted.

The plate is held flush with the top of the subframe with two screws. The screws will shear before they pull out, so the grip is good, and there is no scope for any vertical movement. Fit all the plates.

Lower the subframe onto the underside of the top. Each plate has two slots in it, at 90 degrees to each other. Choose the slot that lies in the direction in which the wood will shrink or swell, and fit the screw in the middle of the slot or at the ends, depending on your estimate of how dry the wood is and whether it will swell or shrink when it is brought indoors. It is safe to assume that the wood will shrink, because central heating dries out everything. Place the screw at the beginning of the slot; it will travel along as the wood contracts.

PLOUGHING A BEAD OR A GROOVE

Choose a suitable bead cutter and adjust the fence. Set the cutter to a minimum cut – it becomes harder work as more of the circumference of the bead is exposed – and tighten the locking nut at that setting.

Start the plane close to the end of the workpiece and run the plane off the end, taking a small shaving. Continue to remove shavings from that end and work backwards (Fig. 8). Each pass removes a longer shaving. The end where you first started will be finished before the other end, and the blade should burnish it as it slides across.

Ploughing a groove is worked in the same way as a bead. It is best to start with short strokes to reduce the danger of contrary grain catching the

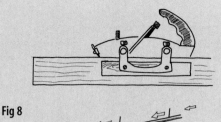

Fig 8

blade. You can usually spot troublesome areas before planing, but this method will give you the best chance of achieving a good finish.

SAWING TENONS

Some of the tenons in this table are quite large and sawing them will take time. To expedite matters, after marking out the shoulders, cut off the shoulders at the ends of the tenons, before scribing the tenon cheeks with the gauge (Fig. 9). The advantage of this

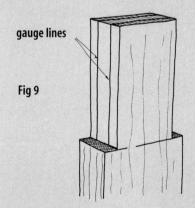

gauge lines

Fig 9

is that the gauge mark is on the tenon, which gives greater accuracy and also ensures that you are not sawing the extra width of the tenon, which will be sawn off later anyway.

Use a rip saw to cut the cheeks and start at a corner with the wood tilted away from you, at an angle that enables you to watch both scribe lines (Fig. 10).

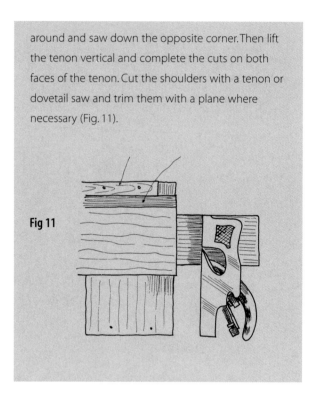

Fig 10

Saw down to the shoulder line, and repeat on the second face of the tenon. Once both faces have been sawn at this 45 degree angle, turn the tenon

around and saw down the opposite corner. Then lift the tenon vertical and complete the cuts on both faces of the tenon. Cut the shoulders with a tenon or dovetail saw and trim them with a plane where necessary (Fig. 11).

Fig 11

CUTTING LIST

Trestle Table (nominal sizes: in/mm)

Item	Quantity	Length	Width	Thickness
Top	4	60/1525	9/230	1¼/32
Pedestal	2	24/610	3½/89	2/50
Subframe				
A	2	45/1145	2½/64	1½/38
B	2	28½/725	2¾/70	2¾/70
C	2	17/430	2¾/70	2¾/70
Pedestal foot				
D	2	7/178	2½/64	2/50
E	2	22/510	2½/64	2/50
Feet	4	5½/140	2½/64	1/25
Stretcher	1	45/1145	3/75	2½/64
Cross supports	2	21/535	2/50	1¼/32

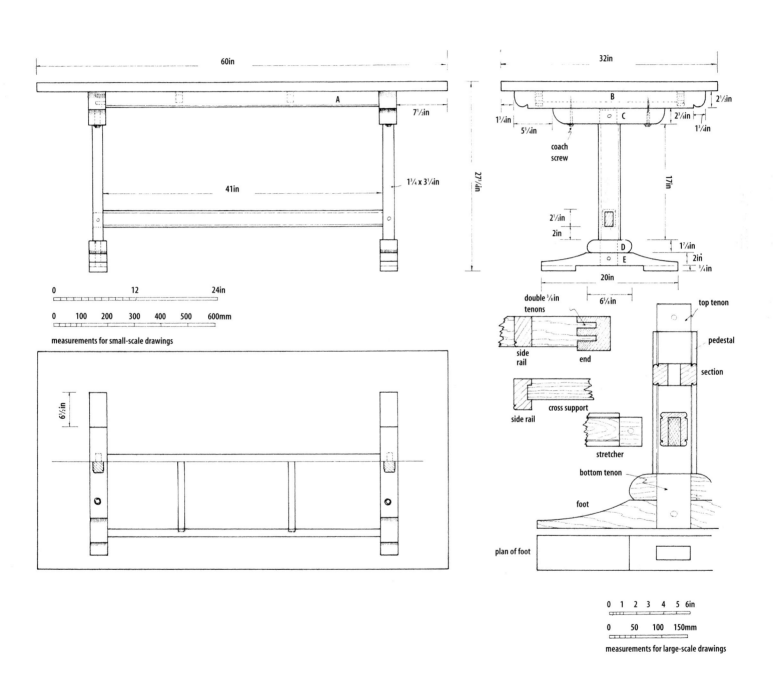

60in

A

7½in

27¼in

41in

1¼ x 3¼in

0   12   24in

0   100   200   300   400   500   600mm

measurements for small-scale drawings

6½in

32in

B

2½in

C

2½in

1¼in

5¾in

1¾in

coach
screw

17in

2½in

2in

D

1⅞in

E

2in

¾in

20in

6⅝in

double ⅜in
tenons

side
rail

end

cross support

side rail

stretcher

top tenon

pedestal

section

bottom tenon

foot

plan of foot

0 1 2 3 4 5 6in

0   50   100   150mm

measurements for large-scale drawings

CORNER CUPBOARD

If you want to make something that gives the impression of quality and craftsmanship but that is easy to construct, choose a corner cupboard. Two-thirds of the cupboard is nailed together, and only the front is joined – and that with mortise and tenon joints. The door is optional, and instructions for making a panelled door can be found on page 131.

This cupboard is made from offcuts of cherrywood. Cherry is a pale, iridescent wood, which is easy to work and gives off a sweet scent when you plane or saw it. The sides and shelves are made

from parana pine, and the front of the shelves are faced with a strip of cherry.

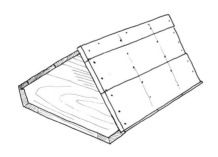

METHOD

You will notice that the corners of the front are formed by two planks glued edge to edge. The outer planks are the returns, which lift the front from the wall and give the piece its appearance of solidity. Built-in corner cupboards usually omit the returns and simply bridge a corner of the room in a straight line. If you find a flat-fronted corner cupboard in an antique shop, it is quite likely to have been obtained from a demolition site or a builder and will show marks of having been stripped and polished.

1 Saw out the pieces for the front framework. It is best if the returns and the adjacent front stile can be sawn from the same plank, so that they can be joined later.

   Mark out and cut the mortise and tenon joints at the corners of the frame, and glue the joints (Fig. 1).

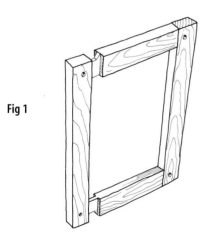

Fig 1

2 Cut the rebates in the outside edge of the returns (see page 9) and plane the bevels on the stiles and the

Fig 2

returns (Fig. 2). For advice on planing see page 36.

   Place the front frame and the two returns face up on the bench, align the ends and tape the joints tightly with parcel tape (Fig. 3).

Fig 3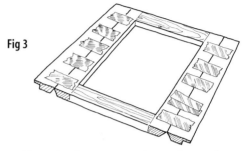

   Turn the frame over and run plenty of PVA adhesive into each joint. Pull the join tight, and hold it together with some rubber bands and more parcel tape (Fig. 4).

Fig 4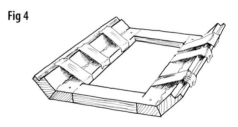

3 When the glue is dry, cut out a cardboard template of the shelves. It is usual to make the angle formed by the back of the cupboard slightly more than 90 degrees so that the cupboard will fit most corners.

   Make up and fit the shelves. They should rest against the stiles and returns. Cut a decorative edge on the two middle shelves (Fig. 5).

Fig 5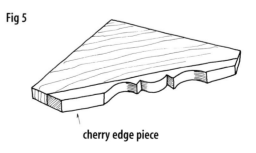

cherry edge piece

Put all four shelves in line on the framework. Sight along them to make sure the sides run true and meet the bottom of the rebate at the edges (Fig. 6), then saw your back planking to length.

Fig 6

Mark on the inside edge of the doorframe the precise positions of each shelf. It will be noticeable if these are even slightly out of square with the frame or the other shelves.

Glue the top and bottom shelves in their exact position, using plywood gussets pinned to the rebate and edge of the top (Fig. 7). Pre-drill through the returns, the top frame and the stiles, and nail them at about 5in (125mm) intervals. Do the same at the bottom.

Fig 7

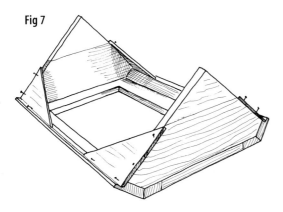

4   Fit the top shelf. Position it exactly on the pencilled marks you made on the framework, glue where it touches the frame and return and hold it with a couple of battens run from the ends, using the plywood gussets to hold the corners, and make a

visual inspection from the front before drilling and nailing it to the sides (Fig. 8).

Fig 8

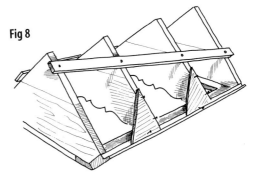

Fit the second shelf in the same way, and then nail on the side planking, overlapping one side with the other at the back (Fig. 9).

Fig 9

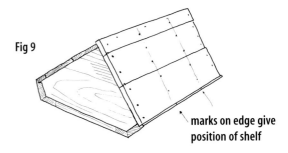

marks on edge give position of shelf

5   Mark off and cut out the moulding strip below the opening, cutting the mitres as described on page 49, and glue and pin it in place (see Tip, page 159).

Make up the bottom moulding, mitre its corners, and fasten.

Cornice return angled slightly downwards.

6 Cut out and fit the cornice (see page 120). Because the sides meet at more than 90 degrees you will have to bisect the angle and mark this off with the sliding bevel (Fig. 10), otherwise the procedures are the same as for the Kitchen Dresser.

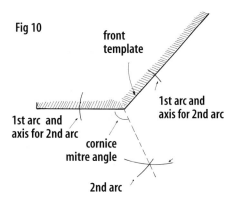

Fig 10

front template

1st arc and axis for 2nd arc

1st arc and axis for 2nd arc

cornice mitre angle

2nd arc

Before nailing the returns, alter the angle slightly so that they dip towards the back. Only a small alteration is required in order to achieve the desired effect. When viewed from below, they should appear to run level (Fig. 11); they should not appear to go up at the ends.

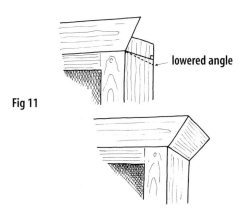

lowered angle

Fig 11

Fit and glue the thin moulding strip immediately beneath the cornice.

7 If you are fitting a door, make it up and fit it now. Hold it in position with some slips of card pushed into the doorframe and drop the H-hinges into place.

Start the holes for the hinges with a bradawl and screw them with brass countersunk screws. Drill a ¼in (6mm) hole on the opposite side of the door for the brass cupboard turn.

When you are happy with your work, remove the brasswork and prepare to finish the cupboard.

FINISHING

Cherry is a pale wood that darkens when exposed to the air. Rather than staining the cupboard with dye, I washed it inside and out with a dilute coat of tannic acid and then fumed it in ammonia (see page 86).

The fuming turned the wood a warm brown, and I then applied a coat of light wood dye – Colron English light oak with a dash of Canadian cedar – to bring out the colour. Almost immediately after, I applied four brush coats of button polish shellac to finish.

After rubbing down with fine 000 wire wool, I replaced the hinges and knob and waxed the whole cupboard.

Finally, I painted the inside planking of the back with home-made paint, made by mixing a blue dry powder pigment colour with some burnt sienna dry colour, using PVA glue as a binder.

TIP

Fine mouldings can be nailed with dressmaking pins. Hardened steel ones are best. Cut them to length with a pair of pliers – close your eyes when you cut or wear safety goggles, because the hardened pins fly off with some force. Hold them with a pair of long-nosed pliers and tap them through the moulding (Fig. 12). If you leave the points just showing on the gluing side, they will help hold the strip steady when they are pressed into place.

Fig 12

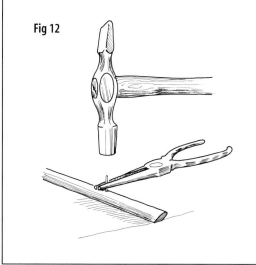

SPECIAL SKILLS

HANGING THE CUPBOARD

Hang the cupboard on the walls using two mirror plates screwed at the top of the back, and one at the bottom. Before you position the plates, hold the cupboard in place and check that the plates are situated where the wall touches the cupboard. Use round-headed screws driven into rawlplugs in the wall to secure it.

CUTTING MOULDINGS WITH A ROUTER

A variety of mouldings are illustrated (Fig. 13). Look after your cutters and hone them sharp before use. The easiest way to cut mouldings is on the edge of a board and then to saw off the finished moulding with the circular saw.

Fig 13

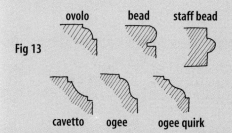

ovolo   bead   staff bead

cavetto   ogee   ogee quirk

Set the cutter in the router and adjust the parallel fence. You may need to alter the fence if you have never used one of the cutters before (Fig. 14).

Fig 14

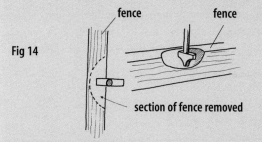

fence   fence

section of fence removed

If the moulding you are planning to cut extends down the full face of the board, tack the board to another straight-edged plank, and plane their edges flush before routing. The lower plank will provide a reliable straightedge after the top plank edge has been trimmed away (Fig. 15).

Fig 15

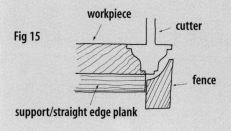

workpiece   cutter

fence

support/straight edge plank

Keep the parallel fence fixed and make several passes along the edge of the board, lowering the cutter each time until it is cutting to its full depth. Always draw the router cutter against its rotation (Fig. 16).

Fig 16

rotation

direction of movement

Once the moulding is formed, carve a wooden block that matches the moulding and sandpaper the moulding smooth. Saw off the moulding when the shaping is complete (Fig. 17).

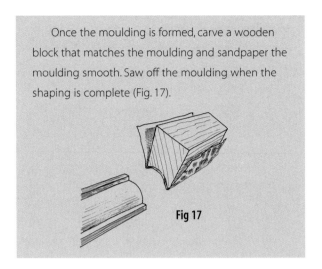

Fig 17

CUTTING LIST

Corner Cupboard (nominal sizes: in/mm)

Item	Quantity	Length	Width	Thickness
Front frame				
Stiles	2	27³/₄/685	2¹/₂/65	1/25
Rails	2	17/430	2¹/₂/65	1/25
Sides	2	27³/₄/685	2¹/₂/65	1/25
Door				
Stiles	2	22³/₄/560	2¹/₂/65	1/25
Rails	2	13/330	2¹/₂/65	1/25
Panel	1	19/485	13¹/₂/345	³/₄/19
Cornice	1	27/685	2¹/₂/65	³/₄/19
	1	24/610	2¹/₂/65	³/₄/19
Mouldings				
Torus bead	1	24/610	¹/₂/12	⁵/₁₆/7
Ovolo bead	1	26/660	³/₄/19	³/₄/19
Shelves				
Capping	4	16¹/₂/420	1/25	³/₄/19
Rest	1	48/1220	10/255	³/₄/19

Back: tongue and groove, 2 panels, each 27 x 14 x ³/₄ in (685 x 356 x 19mm)

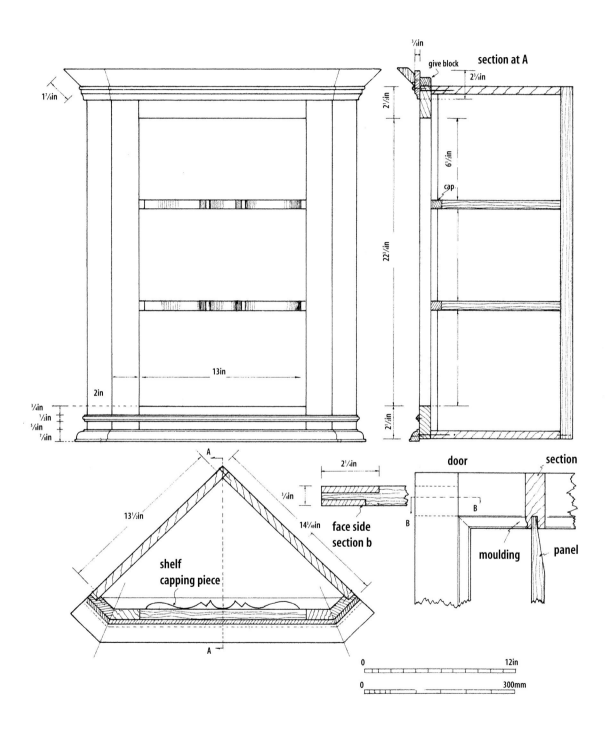

section at A

give block

³⁄₈in

2³⁄₈in

1⁷⁄₈in

2⁷⁄₈in

6³⁄₈in

cap

22³⁄₄in

13in

2in

³⁄₄in
¹⁄₂in
⁵⁄₈in
⁷⁄₈in

2¹⁄₂in

A

13¹⁄₃in

14³⁄₄₆in

2¹⁄₄in

³⁄₄in

face side
section b

shelf
capping piece

A

door

section

B

B

moulding

panel

0   12in

0   300mm

161

SMALL MAHOGANY BOX

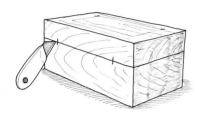

For me, the nice thing about making this little box is that you encounter some very interesting woodworking procedures, without any of the hard work and effort which is associated with bigger projects. And despite this, the finished product is quite beautiful. An additional bonus in this case is that all the components apart from the hinges were offcuts, waiting to be used.

I have described two ways of veneering this box. The end result should be the same, and without any doubt the caul method, using

PVA glue, is the easier. But if you would like to experiment with hammer veneering, I have included some instructions for you to follow. Hammering is quicker and, once you have become accustomed to the process, much more fun.

METHOD

Several features of the box suggest quality. One is the shimmering veneer combined with the way the pieces in the sides are matched to give continuity between the top and the bottom. Another is the ebonized mahogany edging at the lips of the box, which conceal the pine when the box is opened. Solid drawn brass hinges complete the detail. Inside the box is painted.

All the components are machined to size on the circular saw. Fences and guides must be rigid and accurate. For suggestions on ways to improve their accuracy, see page 8.

1 Saw all the pieces to size. The box is glued together before the lid is sawn off, and this guarantees that the lid fits. Because the mahogany strip around the lips of the box makes up the width of the saw cut, the sides can be cut to the width shown in the plans.

2 Cut the four corner lap joints on the saw and fit the ends. Hold the sides together with rubber bands or masking tape and cut the lap joints for the bottom (Fig. 1).

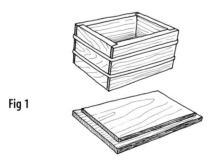

Fig 1

Make the bottom slightly oversize, both at the outside edge, where it should overhang the sides slightly, and also in the centre, where it should fit only when the sides are forced apart. Trim the shoulders of the laps with a rebate plane until the bottom slips neatly into position (Fig. 2).

Fit the top in the same way.

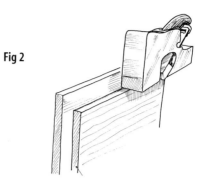

Fig 2

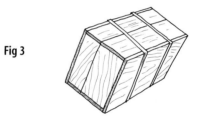

3 The box is nailed and glued together. Before assembling it, mark in pencil around the sides the line where the lid will be sawn off (Fig. 3). When you nail the sides together, avoid driving nails through or near to the line. Drill a small hole through a side to allow air to escape then the box is pushed together.

Fig 3

Glue the sides and bottom together, holding the pieces with panel pins and masking tape. Wipe away glue dribbles before running glue onto the top edges of the box and sliding on the top.

When the glue has hardened, punch down the nails, fill the holes and level the ends and edges of the box with a shoulder plane.

4 Set the saw fence and lower the blade until no more than ¾ in (19mm) is above the table. Saw off the top but do not complete any of these cuts – you should withdraw the box just as the saw is about to reach the tip of the corner. Turn the box around and cut the ends and the other side. Cut through the corners with a tenon saw to release the top.

Plane the corners flat with a shoulder plane, and unless the saw cut is very uneven, leave it. The mahogany strip will cover it, and, despite some unevenness, it will be level.

5 Select a short strip of hardwood – it need not be mahogany; oak or walnut or any quality hardwood will do – and cut it into thin strips to use around the edge of the box. You will find that the simple sawing and planing guide illustrated in Fig. 4 will help you cut the mitres accurately.

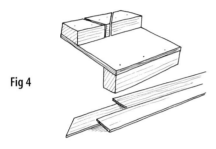

Fig 4

Fit the strips and glue them as they are fitted to avoid confusion. Hold them in position on the lips of the box and lid with masking tape.

When the glue has hardened, plane them smooth, working inwards from the corners. Finish with sandpaper backed to a flat board.

VENEERING

There are several ways of applying the veneer, and I am going to describe two of them – hammer veneering and caul veneering. The box and its lid are veneered separately. Hammer veneering is a traditional way of laying veneer, and you will need to make a few simple tools before you begin. Caul veneering, using PVA, is much more straightforward and you will need some G-clamps and some flat blocks of wood.

Hammer Veneering

You will need to use hot animal glue for hammer veneering. Mix up a sufficient quantity of fresh glue to cover both the surface of the box and the inside face of the veneers. Pour the pearls of glue into the glue pot, cover them with cold water and leave the pearls to swell. After about 12 hours, warm the glue in a double boiler and add just enough water so that glue runs off the brush cleanly and easily. Too much water will weaken the glue but too little will make it difficult to apply.

You will need a cutting board, an electric iron, a straightedge, a knife, some masking tape or clear adhesive tape and a bowl of very hot water. You will also need a veneering hammer, which you can make (Fig. 5), to provide a flat straightedge through which pressure can be applied to the veneer by way of its broad wooden back and handle.

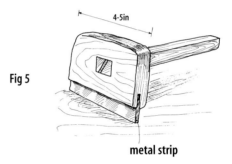

4-5in

Fig 5

metal strip

You will also want a knife and although a craft knife or a bevel-edge chisel held as illustrated in Fig. 6 works quite well, you will probably find that an old steel kitchen knife with tiny teeth sawn into the tip of the blade will be best of all.

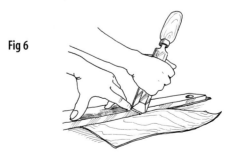

Fig 6

Cut pieces of veneer to about ¼in (6mm) oversize all round. For hammer veneering it is best

if single sheets are used. Made-up sheets of marquetry or built-up patterns are difficult to lay using the hammer and hot glue.

Apply the veneer to the ends first, then the sides and lastly the top. Hold the box in the vice and spread glue liberally onto one end. Apply a generous layer of glue on the inside face of the veneer. It does not matter if the glue chills once it is brushed on, so do not hurry.

When the glue is spread on both pieces, press the veneer onto the box. Switch on the electric iron and set it to a low temperature – it needs only to melt the glue. If it is too hot it will burn the glue. Warm a rag in the bowl of hot water, wring it out and wipe it over the veneer, which makes it easier to move the iron over the surface.

When the iron is warm enough for you to be able to feel its warmth when it is held about 1in (25mm) from your cheek, press it carefully over half of the veneer, moving it gently until the glue melts.

Then, using the hammer, work along the grain, pressing down and working outwards to remove all surplus glue and air bubbles from under the veneer (Fig. 7). Warm the other half and finish laying your first sheet, then, while the glue is still warm, trim the veneer flush with the sides (Fig. 8).

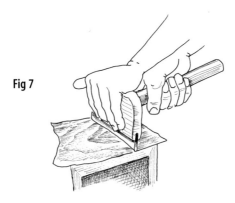

Fig 7

You can now finish the rest of the veneering – ends, sides and, last of all, the top. Scrape or sandpaper the box smooth after the glue has hardened.

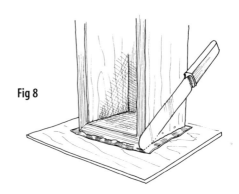

Fig 8

If you find that the veneer won't lie flat, it is probably because the glue is too thin and weak. Alternatively it may have resulted from your having splashed on too much water when you dampened the veneer before using the iron. This will have caused the wood to swell and buckle. Overuse of the iron, particularly if it is too hot, will dry out the glue and impair the glue join.

If the veneer splits or creeps away from the edge, it is probably because you used the iron across the grain rather than with it. This will have caused the iron to stretch the veneer, which will shrink and pull back as it cools.

Caul Veneering

The advantage of caul veneering is that it is easy to use the veneers decoratively to make matched patterns between panels of veneer or to lay areas of marquetry. All you need do is make sure that the veneers are held together with adhesive tape or thin masking tape and are positioned accurately before clamping.

For additional advice on marquetry, cross-banding and shading veneers see my book *The Illustrated Handbook of Furniture Restoration*.

It is easier to use PVA glue rather than animal glue for this method of veneering. You will need a couple of flat boards, one a fraction wider than the sides, and one a fraction wider than the top.

Cut the pieces of veneer to size, joining them

where necessary. Apply plenty of PVA glue to the end of the box and to the veneer. Hold the board so that it overhangs the vice, and wrap the overhanging part with cling film. Lay the veneer, glue side up, on the film, and press the end of the box down onto it. Clamp it tight (Fig. 9). Release the clamps after about three hours – before the glue is quite dry – and trim off the surplus.

Fig 9

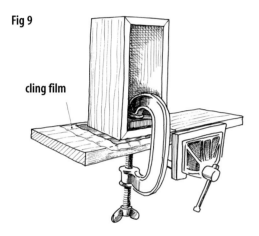

cling film

Veneer the opposite end, and then continue around the sides of the box. When the ends and sides of the lid have been veneered, finish with the top, then sand and scrape the veneers clean and smooth.

FITTING THE STRINGING

Whichever method of veneering you used, you can move straight onto fitting the stringing without waiting for the glue to harden.

Use a steel sand plate to clean up all the corners and edges of the box, but take care that you do not rock it at the corners and always work from the corners inwards.

Mark the position for the stringing with a soft pencil. You can incise the edges of the line with a cutting gauge or with a scalpel and straightedge.

The cutting gauge is the easier tool to use, but if you are going to use a scalpel I find that, on small

work, it is easier to use the back of a new hacksaw blade to guide the scalpel rather than a straightedge, which will sometimes slip (Fig. 10).

Fig 10

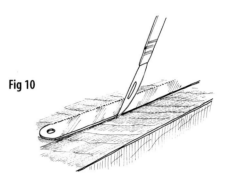

Incise the lines for the stringing and remove the waste from between the lines with a thin chisel. You can make your own chisel by grinding a broken machine hacksaw or jigsaw blade to a satisfactory edge. It is not worth fitting a handle for it, but it might be worth wrapping the rest of the blade in masking tape.

Trim and fit the stringing. Run glue into the groove, pressing the stringing into the groove with the back of a hammer (Fig. 11). Cut the joints as you reach them, marking them with a knife and cutting them with a chisel, placing a piece of veneer between the stringing and the box to protect the box.

Fig 11

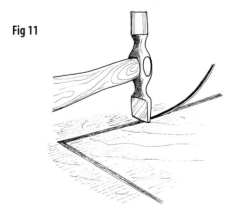

FITTING THE HINGES

Use good quality drawn brass hinges and fix them with ⅜in (10mm) countersunk brass or steel woodscrews.

Put the box and its lid together on the bench, making sure that the top is exactly aligned. Use a sharp pencil to mark across the join the positions of the two hinges. Incise the inside mark for each hinge, letting the knife blade mark snick the top and bottom edges (Fig. 12). You are marking four identical slots – two in the top and two in the base – which have to line up and hold the opposite flanges of the hinges.

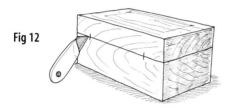

Fig 12

Take off the lid and square the four knife marks across the lip (Fig. 13). Take a hinge and place it in position on the lip. Move it a fraction until it just covers the one line, and nick a mark for the other (Fig. 14). Square this across. Repeat with the other three hinge positions.

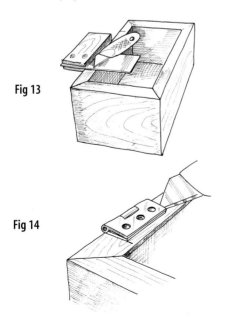

Fig 13

Fig 14

Take a marking or cutting gauge and set it as illustrated in Fig. 15. This is the depth at which the hinge is set into the lip. Take a second gauge, and set it to slightly less than half the hinge thickness and scribe between the lip marks.

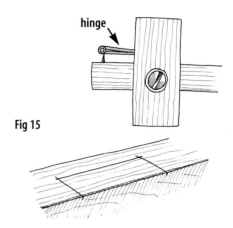

hinge

Fig 15

Take a fine toothed saw – a dovetail saw or a small hack saw will do – and cut across the hinge position. Do not cut below or beyond the gauge marks.

Remove the waste with a keen ¼in (6mm) or ⅜in (10mm) bevel-edge chisel and then cut back the slot to the gauge line and end lines incised in the mahogany (Fig. 16).

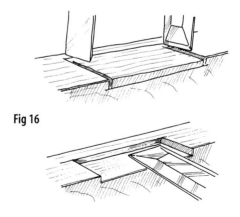

Fig 16

Repeat with the other three hinge positions. Screw the hinges in place, fitting the hinges to the lid first. Hold each hinge with a single screw to check its fit before anchoring it with a second.

If you find that the lid won't shut properly, it may be because the screws are too big and touching. Replace them with smaller gauge screws. If the hinge countersinking is inadequate, bore out the countersink recesses with a countersink bit. If the hinge is recessed too far, fit a slip of veneer under the hinge to raise it slightly.

Another problem may be that the edges of the box are twisted out of alignment. This may be the result of the hinges being recessed into the lip by differing amounts. Check the depths of the recesses with a marking or cutting gauge and refasten incorrectly fitted hinges with new screws driven into fresh holes.

FINISHING

This box has no lock, but I cut and inlaid an ivory escutcheon (made from a piano key), which has a dummy keyhole in it. Special box locks can be obtained from good ironmongers, and to fit them you will need to cut a square recess in the inside front of the box and recess the catch plate into the lip of the box immediately above it. This requires careful marking out, but the cutting of the square recess is accomplished using the same techniques of sawing and chiselling as were used when the hinges were fitted, and the catch bar is inlaid in exactly the same way as the stringing.

I removed the hinges before French polishing the box. The lips of the box were then ebonized and polished.

The flame mahogany was already a fine colour, but I added a tint of Canadian cedar to the English light oak and washed it lightly over the box, leaving it to dry.

I then applied a quick brush coat of button polish shellac, and followed this by an application of grain filler, rubbed into the wood with a coarse rag.

After cleaning off the surplus filler with a rag, I took a wad of cotton wool, about the size of a

tennis ball, formed it into a slightly oval-shaped ball and wrapped it in a twist of cotton sheet (Fig. 17). To charge the rubber, as this is known, with polish, you open the twist, and drop button polish onto the wad from a small bottle.

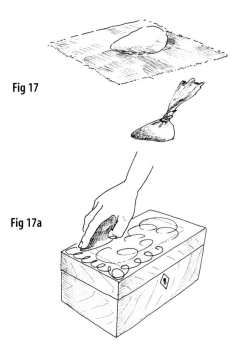

Fig 17

Fig 17a

Pressing gently but increasing the pressure as the rubber dried, I rubbed the polish into the wood. It left an exciting sheen at first, but dried dull. As soon as the rubber was exhausted of polish, I left the box for about 30 minutes for the shellac to sink in and harden.

This was the first stage finished. The shellac hardens in the wood, seals the filler and provides a surface over which the uncovered cotton wool wad can move easily.

Next I poured some button polish into a saucer, removed the wad from the cloth (which I put into a screw-topped jar to keep it clean and damp with polish), and dipped the wad directly into the button polish. With a freshly charged wad (or fad as it is known), I worked quickly over the box, using a regular circular motion (Fig. 17a).

It is important not to stop the fad on the work or it will dissolve the finish. You should start the fad moving before gliding it onto the box and glide it off again before stopping. After each replenishment, start again with a light touch and finish heavy. The early strokes pile on the finish, while the later ones burnish it and press the shellac into the wood.

This is such a small box that you cannot build up much of a finish at a time. It is inadvisable to pile wet polish onto a finish that is already unstable, so after a short while I set the box aside and left the polish to harden.

Several sessions of building up the polish resulted in a satisfactory gloss. I left this to harden, and then lightly sanded it with 240 glasspaper dipped with a little linseed oil.

I then wrapped the wad once again in its cotton twist, recharged it by dripping polish into it as before and worked all over the box with light, swirling figure-of-eight strokes (Fig. 18).

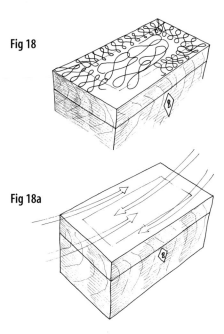

Fig 18

Fig 18a

I recharged the rubber three times before finishing with long light strokes along the grain,

starting and finishing off the box (Fig. 19). By now there was a quite a shine. I left the box to harden for several days, and then rubbed it all over with talcum powder and a little olive oil, using the heel of my palm as a polishing mop.

The mahogany lip to the box is ebonized using Indian ink and then polished with a couple of rubbers of black polish. Brush the Indian ink carefully around the lip of the box, lightly sand it when it is dry, and then mix a small quantity of strong black aniline stain, strain it through a cloth to remove undissolved grains and add a little transparent shellac. Stir for a while, then make up a fresh rubber. Apply the black shellac in long sweeps along the lips of the box.

After two rubbers of polish, leave the shellac to harden before rubbing it down lightly with 000 wire wool.

Refit the hinges, and finished by waxing the box with a brown wax furniture polish.

Problems

When you are polishing you may find that the polish creeps away in small patches (usually in the shape of fingermarks). This is the result of localized greasiness. Wait for the polish to harden and then rub the surface back with 240 grit paper, lubricated with a little linseed oil.

You sometimes find that after building up to a good smooth polish, the final strokes pull the finish into grainy bumps. This is because too much polish has been put on too quickly. Leave the work to harden for a day, then sand it back lightly and continue laying on the polish. Stop before the finish feels rubbery.

If the swirling marks left by the rubber are still obvious after the final long strokes have been completed, too much pressure with a full rubber has caused excessive build-up of ridges. You will have to sand the surface smooth and try again but with a lighter touch.

CUTTING LIST
Small Mahogany Box (nominal sizes: in/mm)

Item	Quantity	Length	Width	Thickness
Side planks	2	$11\frac{1}{2}$/290	6/150	$\frac{3}{4}$/19 Parana pine
End planks	2	$6\frac{1}{2}$/165	6/150	$\frac{3}{4}$/19 Parana pine
Top and bottom	2	$11\frac{1}{2}$/290	7/178	$\frac{3}{4}$/19 Parana pine
Mahogany flame veneer	1 leaf*			
Ebony stringing	1	36/915	$\frac{1}{16}$/1	
Hardwood lipping	1	36/915	$\frac{5}{8}$/16	$\frac{1}{8}$/2 Mahogany offcuts

*Veneers are sold by the leaf

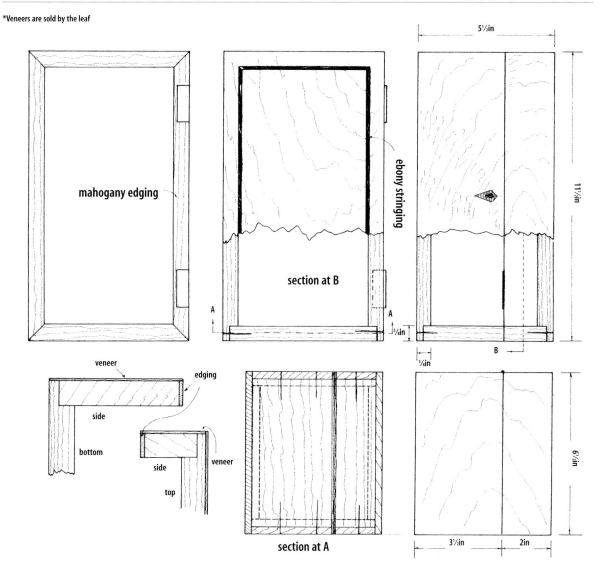

LIST OF SUPPLIERS

UK

TIMBER:

Interesting Timbers
Hazel Farm
Compton Martin
Somerset BS18 6LH
Tel: 01761 463356

North Heigham Sawmills Ltd
Paddock Street
Norwich NR2 4TW
Tel: 01603 622978

Timberman
Gwili Garage
Bronwydd
Carmarthen
Dyfed SA33 6BE
Tel: 01267 232621

TOOLS:

T Brooker & Sons Ltd
39 Bucklersbury
Hitchin
Hertfordshire SG5 1BQ
Tel: 01462 434501

CRM Saw Company Ltd
17 Arnside Road
Waterlooville
Hampshire PO7 7UP
Tel: 01705 255144

Murray's Tool Store
83 Morrison Street
Edinburgh EH3 8BU
Tel: 0131 229 1577

WJT Crafts and Woodturning Supplies
New Farm Road Industrial Estate
Prospect Road
New Alresford
Hampshire SO24 9QF
Tel: 01962 735411

RAWHIDE:

Tandy Leathercraft Ltd
Billing Park
Northampton NN3 4BG
Tel: 01604 407177

BRASSWARE:

Martin and Company
97 Camden Street
Birmingham B1 3DG
Tel: 0121 233 2111

John Lawrence and Co (Dover) Ltd
Granville Street
Dover
Kent CT16 2LF
Tel: 01304 201425

Sargent's Tools
44-52 Oxford Road
Reading
Berks RG1 7LH
Tel: 01734 586522

ROUTER CUTTERS:

Trend Machinery and Cutting Tools Ltd
Unit 'N' Penfold Works
Imperial Way
Watford
Hertfordshire WD2 4YF
Tel: 01923 249911

CABINETMAKERS' SUPPLIES:

Fiddes and Son
Florence Works
Brindley Road
Cardiff CF1 7TX
Tel: 01222 340323

CANE AND RUSH:

Touchwood Craft Centre
15 Warminster Road
Westbury
Wiltshire BA13 3PD
Tel: 01373 823381

REPRODUCTION IRONWORK:

David Tigwell
Ladywood Cottage
Watledge
Nailsworth
Gloucester GL6 OBB
Tel: 01453 832954

USA

TIMBER:

Maurice L Condon Co Inc.
248 Ferris Avenue
White Plains
NY 10603

TOOLS:

Frog Tool Co Ltd
700 W Jackson Boulevard
Chicago
Illinois 60606

Garrett Wade Company
161 Avenue of the Americas
New York
New York 10013

Woodcraft Supply Corp.
41 Atlantic Avenue
Box 4000
Woburn
Massachusetts 01888
(also hinges, brassware, fiber rush,
finishing materials)

FINISHING SUPPLIES:

Garrett Wade Company
(see address above)

**Mohawk Finishing
Products Inc.**
Amsterdam
New York 12010

BRASSWARE:

Ball and Ball
463 West Lincoln Highway
Exton
Pennsylvania 19341

CANE AND RUSH:

The Woodworker's Store
21801 Industrial Blvd.
Rogers
Minnesota 55374

LEATHER:

Roberts Leather Studios Inc.
214 West 29th Street
Unit 403
New York
New York 10001

Berman Leathercraft Inc.
145 South Street
Boston
Massachusetts 0211

CANADA

RAWHIDE:

Tandy Leather Company
PO Box 13000
Barrie
Ontario
L4M 4W4

FURTHER READING

George Buchanan, *Country Furniture for the Home: The Kitchen*, Cassell, 1995

George Buchanan, *Country Furniture for the Home: The Living Room*, Cassell, 1996

George Buchanan, *Garden Furniture: A Practical Guide for Woodworkers*, Cassell 1991

George Buchanan, *The Illustrated Handbook of Furniture Restoration*, BT Batsford Ltd, London, 1985

Thomas Corkhill, *A Glossary of Wood*, Stobart and Son Ltd, London, 1988

H E Desch, *Timber: Its Structure, Properties and Utilisation*, Macmillan, London, 1985

Mark Duginske, *Mastering Woodworking Machines*, The Taunton Press, 1992

Mark Finney, *The Stanley Book of Woodwork*, BT Batsford, 1994

Franklin Gottshall, *How to Design and Construct Period Furniture*, Bonanza, 1989

Wolfram Graubner, *Woodworking Joints*, BT Batsford Ltd, London, 1992

Charles Hayward, *Staining and Polishing*, Unwin Hyman, London, 1988

R Bruce Hoadley, *Understanding Wood*, The Taunton Press, 1980

R Bruce Hoadley, *Identifying Wood*, The Taunton Press, 1990

GLOSSARY

Adze A variation of the axe, with a curved blade set at right angles to the shaft. Used for smoothing and gouging timber.

Angle bevel An adjustable try square.

Annual rings Concentric rings of woody fibre, revealed in a cross section of a tree trunk. Each ring represents one year's growth. The paler, softer rings are spring growth and the darker and harder rings are slow summer growth.

Apron rail Decorative horizontal board.

Armoire Large cupboard (French).

Arris Corner or sharp edge.

Astragel A semi-circular, projecting moulding.

Auger A large diameter drill bit, operated with two hands.

Badger Wide rebate plane with its iron set on the skew.

Bare faced tenon Tenon with a shoulder on one side only.

Bead A small, semi-circular sectioned moulding.

Bench hook A board used to steady work when sawing or chiselling.

Bench screw A wooden vice.

Bevel A flat surface other than at right angles or square, occupying the full width of the wood.

Bine The raised part of a spiral turning.

Bit Any boring tool that fits into a hand brace.

Block plane Small plane with a blade set at a low angle. Also heavy plane used in conjunction with a shooting board.

Bow saw A narrow bladed frame saw, used with both hands for making curved sawcuts.

Bracket foot A foot made from two flat boards, shaped and joined with a mitre.

Bradawl A pointed boring tool for starting small diameter screws and small nails.

Bullnose Small metal plane for working into tight corners.

Butt hinge A plain hinge that is recessed into the door and frame.

Butt joint A plain joint where the joining pieces are at 90 degrees to each other.

Carcase Outer structural framework of a piece of furniture, usually of flat boards.

Cast A wind or a twist in a board.

Caul A flat panel used to press down veneers that are being glued.

Cavetto A hollow moulding.

Cheek Side of a mortice and the part removed to form a tenon.

Champher An angle planed on the corner of a piece of wood.

Clamp A strip of wood set flush and at right angles to a wide board to hold it flat.

Coach screw Large, square headed wood screw tightened with a spanner.

Cock bead A raised small sectioned bead.

Cornice Decorative moulding at the top of a piece of furniture.

Countersunk A flush headed screw.

Crossbanding A veneered strip, usually at the edge of the board, and with its grain perpendicular to the edge.

Curl Decorative figure obtained from the junction between the trunk and a large branch.

Cupshake A fault in timber where timber splits, separating the annual rings.

Deal General term for fir.

Dentils Decorative square blocks used to ornament a cornice or moulding.

Doatiness Decaying timber, discoloured by red flecks.

Draw knife Two handed knife, used with the grain.

Dressed stuff Timber that is planed.

Druxiness Fungal decay, associated with damaged parts of a trunk, indicated by patchy bleached areas.

Ear piece A part of a decorative feature, carved from a separate block.

Ebonise To blacken with stain and polish.

Escutcheon A metal or other plate surrounding a keyhole.

Extension bit A bit with an adjustable spur to cut various sized holes.

Face mark Pencilled mark used to identify trued up working surface.

Feather tongue A thin, cross grain tongue used to edge join boards.

Fielded panel A panel with a raised centre.

Figure Particularly decorative wood grain.

Fox wedged A secret wedge, concealed within the joint.

Foxiness A decay in oak, marked by reddish tinge.

Gauge Marking tool used for lines parallel to an edge.

Graining Decorative painted finish, simulating wood.

Groundwork Wooden panel to which veneer is applied.

Halving joint A joint where each piece is reduced in thickness to accommodate the other and fit flush.

Haunch A projection at the edge of a tenon, usually to fill a groove or strengthen a tenon.

Heartwood The harder, older timber in the centre of the trunk.

Herring bone Decorative inlay, composed of two diagonally cut strips joined to form an arrow head grain pattern.

Holdfast A bench clamp anchored in a hole in the bench to hold the workpiece.

Housing To recess one piece of wood into another without reducing its thickness.

Inlay Decorative patterns recessed flush into a surface.

Iron Cutting blade of a machine or hand tools – usually applied to planes.

Kerf The saw cut, wider than the saw blade due to its set.

Key A piece of wood recessed into a plank, to hold a join, or to bridge a split, to prevent movement.

Laminating Thin planks joined by glue to make a single piece. Often used in curved work, and for strength.

Lapped dovetail A dovetail joint where the joint is concealed on one side (as used in drawer fronts).

Lapped joint Where one plank is rebated to hold another.

Lipped drawer A drawer that overlaps the carcase.

Live knot A knot in a piece of timber that is secure. Those with black (bark) circling them will usually loosen and fall out.

Loose seat An upholstered insert into a chair frame.

Marking knife A sharp, fine-bladed knife for incising shoulder lines.

Match boards Tongue and grooved boards.

Medullary rays Radiating rays through a trunk, carrying food substances inwards or outwards through a living trunk, or serving as storage tissue. Often very decorative, as in oak, sycamore, maple and beech.

Mitre In picture and panel framing, a joint where the edges join at 45 degrees to each other. Generally, a plane joint where the surfaces meet at an angle of other than 90 degrees.

Mitre box An open-ended box or trough, incorporating saw guides at 45 degrees.

Mitre dovetail A secret dovetail, often found at the tops of bureau and high quality cabinets.

Mitre square A try square with its blade set at 45 degrees.

Mortise and tenon A joint consisting of a mortise or recess, and a tenon which fits tightly in it.

Munting or muntin An internal vertical framing member. Also used to refer to the support fitted in the centre of a wide drawer to support the bottom.

Ogee A serpentine sectioned moulding, consisting of reversed arcs.

Oilstone A fine grained stone used for sharpening edge tools.

Ovolo A moulding of quarter circle or elliptical section.

Oyster shell A high quality veneering pattern using veneers sliced across a trunk, often walnut or laburnum.

Parting tool A V shaped gouge.

Pedestal A square raised base to support a desk or cupboard.

Pellet A turned wooden plug to conceal a screw or bolt head.

Pigeon hole A small compartment for storing papers, as in the interior fittings of a bureau.

Pinned joint Where pins or dowels are used to secure a mortise.

Pins Part of a dovetail joint where the dovetails slot between them.

Plough plane A grooving plane.

Pot board A low shelf to a dresser or cupboard.

Pot life The length of time in which glue remains usable.

Punch A tapered steel driver for sinking nail heads.

Quartered wood Logs cut into quarters and then cut radially. In oak, such a board would display its medullary rays and would be termed wainscot oak.

Quirk A narrow groove beside a bead.

Rail A horizontal framing member.

Rake The angle at which a chair back slopes.

Reaction timber Timber that has grown in difficult, often steeply sloping, conditions displays faults when it is converted. There will usually be a wandering heart (see below), and on one side there will be tension wood (grown on the uphill side to counteract a tendency to lean), which will shrink and twist. Compression timber (downhill side) is dense but weak.

Rebate A rectangular sinking on the edge of a board or frame.

Return The moulding which is repeated on two adjacent faces and meets.

Riffler A bent rasp used by carvers.

Sapwood Portion of tree through which sap travels upwards, between bark and heartwood. Often soft and weak, readily attacked by worm and beetle.

Scantling The size of the timber.

Scarfe A joint used to extend the length of timber.

Scotia A hollow moulding.

Scratch stock A versatile scraping tool used for working mouldings. Mild steel blade, often filed in the workshop which works on the pulling and pushing strokes.

Secret nailing Nailing through the edge of the board, so that the nail heads are not seen.

Set Inclination given to the teeth of a saw to prevent it binding.

Shake A longitudinal split in a log.

Sinking A recessed part of a board.

Skew nailed Nails driven at angles to increase their hold.

Slash sawn Timber sawn through and through, giving a variety of boards, some of good quality, others less so.

Stile Vertical framing member.

Strap hinge Long hinge fixed on the surface of the board.

Stub tenon One that does not pass through the mortised piece.

Stuck moulding One worked in the solid plank.

Tambour A sliding door made of thin strips of wood, joined behind by fabric, and the ends sliding in matching grooves.

Template A pattern.

Tenon The projecting part of the mortise and tenon joint.

Thumb plane A small plane.

Tongue A slip of wood which fits into matching grooves to form edge joints. A loose tongue is a strip that fits into grooves cut in both edges of the pieces being joined.

Veneer A thin, usually decorative, sheet of wood. Sold by the leaf.

Wandering heart A timber defect where the heartwood deviates from the centre of the plank. Often indicates poor weak reaction timber.

Warping Twisting of a board over its width.

Wind Twisting of a board over its length.

Winding sticks Two parallel sticks placed on the ends of the board to sight for wind.

INDEX